World Medical Association

# Medical Ethics Manual

This Manual is a publication of the Ethics Unit of the World
Medical Association. It was written by John R. Williams,
Director of Ethics, WMA. Its contents do not necessarily reflect
the policies of the WMA, except where this is clearly and
explicitly indicated.

Cover, layout and concept by Tuuli Sauren,
Inspirit International Advertising, Belgium.
Production and concept
World Health Communication Associates, UK.

Pictures by Van Parys Media/CORBIS

Cataloguing-in-Publication Data
Williams, John R. (John Reynold), 1942-.
Medical ethics manual.

1. Bioethics 2. Physician-Patient Relations - ethics.
3. Physician's Role  4. Biomedical Research - ethics
5. Interprofessional Relations 6. Education, Medical - ethics
7. Case reports 8. Manuals I. Title

ISBN 92-990028-0-0
(NLM classification: W 50)

# TABLE OF CONTENTS

# ACKNOWLEDGMENTS

The WMA Ethics Unit is profoundly grateful to the following individuals for providing extensive and thoughtful comments on earlier drafts of this Manual:

*Prof. Solly Benatar*, University of Cape Town, South Africa

*Prof. Kenneth Boyd*, University of Edinburgh, Scotland

*Dr. Annette J. Braunack-Mayer*, University of Adelaide, Australia

*Dr. Robert Carlson*, University of Edinburgh, Scotland

*Mr. Sev Fluss, WMA and CIOMS*, Geneva, Switzerland

*Prof. Eugenijus Gefenas*, University of Vilnius, Lithuania

*Dr. Delon Human, WMA*, Ferney-Voltaire, France

*Dr. Girish Bobby Kapur*, George Washington University, Washington, DC, USA

*Prof. Nuala Kenny*, Dalhousie University, Halifax, Canada

*Prof. Cheryl Cox Macpherson*, St. George's University, Grenada

*Ms. Mareike Moeller*, Medizinische Hochschule Hannover, Germany

*Prof. Ferenc Oberfrank*, Hungarian Academy of Sciences, Budapest, Hungary

*Mr. Atif Rahman*, Khyber Medical College, Peshawar, Pakistan

*Mr. Mohamed Swailem*, Banha Faculty of Medicine, Banha, Egypt, and his ten fellow students who identified vocabulary that was not familiar to individuals whose first language is other than English.

*The WMA Ethics Unit is supported in part by an unrestricted educational grant from Johnson & Johnson.*

# FOREWORD

*Dr. Delon Human*
*Secretary General*
*World Medical Association*

It is incredible to think that although the founders of medical ethics, such as Hippocrates, published their works more than 2000 years ago, the medical profession, up until now, has not had a basic, universally used, curriculum for the teaching of medical ethics. This first WMA Ethics Manual aims to fill that void. What a privilege it is to introduce it to you!

The Manual's origin dates back to the 51st World Medical Assembly in 1999. Physicians gathered there, representing medical associations from around the world, decided, "to strongly recommend to Medical Schools worldwide that the teaching of Medical Ethics and Human Rights be included as an obligatory course in their curricula." In line with that decision, a process was started to develop a basic teaching aid on medical ethics for all medical students and physicians that would be based on WMA policies, but not be a policy document itself. This Manual, therefore, is the result of a comprehensive global developmental and consultative process, guided and coordinated by the WMA Ethics Unit.

Modern healthcare has given rise to extremely complex and multifaceted ethical dilemmas. All too often physicians are unprepared to manage these competently. This publication is specifically structured to reinforce and strengthen the ethical mindset and practice of physicians and provide tools to find ethical solutions to these dilemmas. It is not a list of "rights and wrongs" but an attempt to sensitise the conscience of the physician, which is the basis for all sound and ethical decision-making. To this end, you will find several case studies in the book, which are intended to foster individual ethical reflection as well as discussion within team settings.

As physicians, we know what a privilege it is to be involved in the patient-physician relationship, a unique relationship which facilitates an exchange of scientific knowledge and care within a framework of ethics and trust. The Manual is structured to address issues related to the different relationships in which physicians are involved, but at the core will always be the patient-physician relationship. In recent times, this relationship has come under pressure due to resource constraints and other factors, and this Manual shows the necessity of strengthening this bond through ethical practice.

Finally, a word on the centrality of the patient in any discussion on medical ethics. Most medical associations acknowledge in their foundational policies that ethically, the best interests of the individual patient should be the first consideration in any decision on care. This WMA Ethics Manual will only serve its purpose well if it helps prepare medical students and physicians to better navigate through the many ethical challenges we face in our daily practice and find effective ways **TO PUT THE PATIENT FIRST**.

# INTRODUCTION

## WHAT IS MEDICAL ETHICS?

Consider the following medical cases, which could have taken place in almost any country:

1.  Dr. P, an experienced and skilled surgeon, is about to finish night duty at a medium-sized community hospital. A young woman is brought to the hospital by her mother, who leaves immediately after telling the intake nurse that she has to look after her other children. The patient is bleeding vaginally and is in a great deal of pain. Dr. P examines her and decides that she has had either a miscarriage or a self-induced abortion. He does a quick dilatation and curettage and tells the nurse to ask the patient whether she can afford to stay in the hospital until it is safe for her to be discharged. Dr. Q comes in to replace Dr. P, who goes home without having spoken to the patient.

2.  Dr. S is becoming increasingly frustrated with patients who come to her either before or after consulting another health practitioner for the same ailment. She considers this to be a waste of health resources as well as counter-productive for the health of the patients. She decides to tell these patients that she will no longer treat them if they continue to see other practitioners for the same ailment. She intends to approach her national medical association to lobby the government to prevent this form of misallocation of healthcare resources.

3.  Dr. C, a newly appointed *anaesthetist* in a city hospital, is alarmed by the behaviour of the senior surgeon in the operating room. The surgeon uses out-of-date techniques that prolong operations and result in greater post-operative pain and longer recovery times. Moreover, he makes frequent crude jokes about

Words written in *italics* are defined in the glossary (Appendix A).

the patients that obviously bother the assisting nurses. As a more junior staff member, Dr. C is reluctant to criticize the surgeon personally or to report him to higher authorities. However, he feels that he must do something to improve the situation.

4. Dr. R, a general practitioner in a small rural town, is approached by a contract research organization (C.R.O.) to participate in a clinical trial of a new non-steroidal anti-inflammatory drug (NSAID) for osteoarthritis. She is offered a sum of money for each patient that she enrols in the trial. The C.R.O. representative assures her that the trial has received all the necessary approvals, including one from an ethics review committee. Dr. R has never participated in a trial before and is pleased to have this opportunity, especially with the extra money. She accepts without inquiring further about the scientific or ethical aspects of the trial.

Each of these case studies invites ethical reflection. They raise questions about *physician* **behaviour** and **decision-making** – not scientific or technical questions such as how to treat diabetes or how to perform a double bypass, but questions about *values*, rights and responsibilities. Physicians face these kinds of questions just as often as scientific and technical ones.

In medical practice, no matter what the specialty or the setting, some questions are much easier to answer than others. Setting a simple fracture and suturing a simple laceration pose few challenges to physicians who are accustomed to performing these procedures. At the other end of the spectrum, there can be great uncertainty or disagreement about how to treat some diseases, even common ones such as tuberculosis and hypertension. Likewise, ethical questions in medicine are not all equally challenging. Some are relatively easy to answer, mainly because there is a well-developed *consensus* on the right way to act in the situation (for example, the physician should always ask for a patient's consent to serve as a research subject). Others are much more difficult, especially those for which no consensus has developed or where all the alternatives have drawbacks (for example, rationing of scarce healthcare resources).

So, what exactly is ethics and how does it help physicians deal with such questions? Put simply, ethics is the study of morality – careful and systematic reflection on and analysis of moral decisions and behaviour, whether past, present or future. Morality is the value dimension of human decision-making and behaviour. The language of morality includes nouns such as 'rights', 'responsibilities' and '*virtues*' and adjectives such as 'good' and 'bad' (or 'evil'), 'right' and 'wrong', 'just' and 'unjust'. According to these definitions, ethics is primarily a matter of **knowing** whereas morality is a matter of **doing**. Their close relationship consists in the concern of ethics to provide rational criteria for people to decide or behave in some ways rather than others.

> "...ethics is the study of morality – careful and systematic reflection on and analysis of moral decisions and behaviour"

Since ethics deals with all aspects of human behaviour and decision-making, it is a very large and complex field of study with many branches or subdivisions. The focus of this Manual is **medical ethics,** the branch of ethics that deals with moral issues in medical practice. Medical ethics is closely related, but not identical to, *bioethics* (*biomedical ethics*). Whereas medical ethics focuses primarily on issues arising out of the practice of medicine, bioethics is a very broad subject that is concerned with the moral issues raised by developments in the biological sciences more generally. Bioethics also differs from medical ethics insofar as it does not require the acceptance of certain traditional values that, as we will see in Chapter Two, are fundamental to medical ethics.

As an academic discipline, medical ethics has developed its own specialized vocabulary, including many terms that have been borrowed from philosophy. This Manual does not presuppose any familiarity with philosophy in its readers, and therefore definitions of key terms are provided either where they occur in the text or in the glossary at the end of the Manual.

## WHY STUDY MEDICAL ETHICS?

"As long as the physician is a knowledgeable and skilful clinician, ethics doesn't matter."

"Ethics is learned in the family, not in medical school."

"Medical ethics is learned by observing how senior physicians act, not from books or lectures."

"Ethics is important, but our curriculum is already too crowded and there is no room for ethics teaching."

These are some of the common reasons given for not assigning ethics a major role in the medical school curriculum. Each of them is partially, but only partially, valid. Increasingly throughout the world medical schools are realising that they need to provide their students with adequate time and resources for learning ethics. They have received strong encouragement to move in this direction from organizations such as the World Medical Association and the World Federation for Medical Education (cf. Appendix C).

The importance of ethics in medical education will become apparent throughout this Manual. To summarize, ethics is and always has been an essential component of medical practice. Ethical principles such as respect for persons, informed consent and confidentiality are basic to the physician-patient relationship. However, the application of these principles in specific situations is often problematic, since physicians, patients, their family members and other healthcare personnel may disagree about what is the right way to act in a situation. The study of ethics prepares medical students to recognize difficult situations and to deal with them in a rational and principled manner. Ethics is also important in physicians' interactions with society and their colleagues and for the conduct of medical research.

> "The study of ethics prepares medical students to recognize difficult situations and to deal with them in a rational and principled manner."

## MEDICAL ETHICS, MEDICAL PROFESSIONALISM, HUMAN RIGHTS AND LAW

As will be seen in Chapter One, ethics has been an integral part of medicine at least since the time of Hippocrates, the fifth century B.C.E. (before the Christian era) Greek physician who is regarded as a founder of medical ethics. From Hippocrates came the concept of medicine as a **profession**, whereby physicians make a public promise that they will place the interests of their patients above their own interests (cf. Chapter Three for further explanation). The close relationship of ethics and professionalism will be evident throughout this Manual.

In recent times medical ethics has been greatly influenced by developments in **human rights**. In a *pluralistic* and multicultural world, with many different moral traditions, the major international human rights agreements can provide a foundation for medical ethics that is acceptable across national and cultural boundaries. Moreover, physicians frequently have to deal with medical problems resulting from violations of human rights, such as forced migration and torture. And they are greatly affected by the debate over whether healthcare is a human right, since the answer to this question in any particular country determines to a large extent who has access to medical care. This Manual will give careful consideration to human rights issues as they affect medical practice.

Medical ethics is also closely related to **law**. In most countries there are laws that specify how physicians are required to deal with ethical issues in patient care and research. In addition, the medical licensing and regulatory officials in each country can and do punish physicians for ethical violations. But ethics and law are not identical. Quite often ethics prescribes higher standards of behaviour than does the law, and occasionally ethics requires that physicians disobey laws that demand unethical behaviour. Moreover, laws differ significantly from one country to another while ethics is applicable across national boundaries. For this reason, the focus of this Manual is on ethics rather than law.

> "...often ethics prescribes higher standards of behaviour than does the law, and occasionally ethics requires that physicians disobey laws that demand unethical behaviour"

# CONCLUSION

Medicine is both a science and an art. Science deals with what can be observed and measured, and a competent physician recognizes the signs of illness and disease and knows how to restore good health. But scientific medicine has its limits, particularly in regard to human individuality, culture, religion, freedom, rights and responsibilities. The art of medicine involves the application of medical science and technology to individual patients, families and communities, no two of which are identical. By far the major part of the differences among individuals, families and communities is non-physiological, and it is in recognizing and dealing with these differences that the arts, humanities and social sciences, along with ethics, play a major role. Indeed, ethics itself is enriched by the insights and data of these other disciplines; for example, a theatrical presentation of a clinical dilemma can be a more powerful stimulus for ethical reflection and analysis than a simple case description.

This Manual can provide only a basic introduction to medical ethics and some of its central issues. It is intended to give you an appreciation of the need for continual reflection on the ethical dimension of medicine, and especially on how to deal with the ethical issues that you will encounter in your own practice. A list of resources is provided in Appendix B to help you deepen your knowledge of this field.

# CHAPTER ONE –
# PRINCIPAL FEATURES OF MEDICAL ETHIC:

**A Day in the Life of a French General Practitioner**
© Gilles Fonlupt/Corbis

## OBJECTIVES

After working through this chapter you should be able to:

· explain why ethics is important to medicine
· identify the major sources of medical ethics
· recognize different approaches to ethical decision-making, including your own.

## WHAT'S SPECIAL ABOUT MEDICINE?

Throughout almost all of recorded history and in virtually every part of the world, being a physician has meant something special. People come to physicians for help with their most pressing needs – relief from pain and suffering and restoration of health and well-being. They allow physicians to see, touch and manipulate every part of their bodies, even the most intimate. They do this because they trust their physicians to act in their best interests.

> "Many physicians feel that they are no longer as respected as they once were."

The status of physicians differs from one country to another and even within countries. In general, though, it seems to be deteriorating. Many physicians feel that they are no longer as respected as they once were. In some countries, control of healthcare has moved steadily away from physicians to professional managers and bureaucrats, some of whom tend to see physicians as obstacles to rather than partners in healthcare reforms. Patients who used to accept physicians' orders unquestioningly sometimes ask physicians to defend their recommendations if these are different from advice obtained from other health practitioners or the Internet. Some procedures that formerly only physicians were capable of performing are now done by medical technicians, nurses or paramedics.

Despite these changes impinging on the status of physicians, medicine continues to be a profession that is highly valued by the sick people who need its services. It also continues to attract large numbers of the most gifted, hard-working and dedicated students. In order to meet

> "...to meet the expectations of both patients and students, it is important that physicians know and exemplify the core values of medicine"

the expectations of both patients and students, it is important that physicians know and exemplify the core values of medicine, especially compassion, competence and autonomy. These values, along with respect for fundamental human rights, serve as the foundation of medical ethics.

## WHAT'S SPECIAL ABOUT MEDICAL ETHICS?

Compassion, competence and autonomy are not exclusive to medicine. However, physicians are expected to exemplify them to a higher degree than other people, including members of many other professions.

**Compassion**, defined as understanding and concern for another person's distress, is essential for the practice of medicine. In order to deal with the patient's problems, the physician must identify the symptoms that the patient is experiencing and their underlying causes and must want to help the patient achieve relief. Patients respond better to treatment if they perceive that the physician appreciates their concerns and is treating them rather than just their illness.

A very high degree of **competence** is both expected and required of physicians. A lack of competence can result in death or serious morbidity for patients. Physicians undergo a long training period to ensure competence, but considering the rapid advance of medical knowledge, it is a continual challenge for them to maintain their competence. Moreover, it is not just their scientific knowledge and technical skills that they have to maintain but their ethical knowledge, skills and attitudes as well, since new ethical issues arise with changes in medical practice and its social and political environment.

**Autonomy**, or self-determination, is the core value of medicine that has changed the most over the years. Individual physicians have traditionally enjoyed a high degree of clinical autonomy in deciding how to treat their patients. Physicians collectively (the medical profession) have been free to determine the standards of medical education and medical practice. As will be evident throughout this

## THE WORLD MEDICAL ASSOCIATION DECLARATION OF GENEVA

At the time of being admitted as a member of the medical profession:

I solemnly pledge myself to consecrate my life to the service of humanity;

I will give to my teachers the respect and gratitude which is their due;

I will practise my profession with conscience and dignity;

The health of my patient will be my first consideration;

I will respect the secrets which are confided in me, even after the patient has died;

I will maintain by all the means in my power, the honour and the noble traditions of the medical profession;

My colleagues will be my sisters and brothers;

I will not permit considerations of age, disease or disability, creed, ethnic origin, gender, nationality, political affiliation, race, sexual orientation, or social standing to intervene between my duty and my patient;

I will maintain the utmost respect for human life from its beginning even under threat and I will not use my medical knowledge contrary to the laws of humanity;

I make these promises solemnly, freely and upon my honour.

Manual, both of these ways of exercising physician autonomy have been moderated in many countries by governments and other authorities imposing controls on physicians. Despite these challenges, physicians still value their clinical and professional autonomy and try to preserve it as much as possible. At the same time, there has been a widespread acceptance by physicians worldwide of patient autonomy, which means that patients should be the ultimate decision-makers in matters that affect themselves. This Manual will deal with examples of potential conflicts between physician autonomy and respect for patient autonomy.

Besides its adherence to these three core values, medical ethics differs from the general ethics applicable to everyone by being publicly *professed* in an oath such as the World Medical Association **Declaration of Geneva** and/or a code. Oaths and codes vary from one country to another and even within countries, but they have many common features, including promises that physicians will consider the interests of their patients above their own, will not discriminate against patients on the basis of race, religion or other human rights grounds, will protect the confidentiality of patient information and will provide emergency care to anyone in need.

## WHO DECIDES WHAT IS ETHICAL?

Ethics is *pluralistic*. Individuals disagree among themselves about what is right and what is wrong, and even when they agree, it can be for different reasons. In some societies, this disagreement is regarded as normal and there is a great deal of freedom to act however one wants, as long as it does not violate the rights of others. In more traditional societies, however, there is greater agreement on ethics and greater social pressure, sometimes backed by laws, to act in certain ways rather than others. In such societies culture and religion often play a dominant role in determining ethical behaviour.

The answer to the question, "who decides what is ethical for people in general?" therefore varies from one society to another and even within the same society. In liberal societies, individuals have a great deal of freedom to decide for themselves what is ethical, although they will likely be influenced by their families, friends, religion, the media and other external sources. In more traditional societies, family and clan elders, religious authorities and political leaders usually have a greater role than individuals in determining what is ethical.

Despite these differences, it seems that most human beings can agree on some fundamental ethical principles, namely, the basic human rights proclaimed in the United Nations **Universal Declaration of Human Rights** and other widely accepted and officially endorsed documents. The human rights that are especially important for medical ethics include the right to life, to freedom from discrimination, torture and cruel, inhuman or degrading treatment, to freedom of opinion and expression, to equal access to public services in one's country, and to medical care.

For physicians, the question, "who decides what is ethical?" has until recently had a somewhat different answer than for people in general. Over the centuries the medical profession has developed its own standards of behaviour for its members, which are expressed in codes of ethics and related policy documents. At the global level, the WMA has set forth a broad range of ethical statements that specify the behaviour required of physicians no matter where they live and practise. In many, if not most, countries medical associations have been responsible for developing and enforcing the applicable ethical standards. Depending on the country's approach to medical law, these standards may have legal status.

The medical profession's privilege of being able to determine its own ethical standards has never been absolute, however. For example:

- Physicians have always been subject to the general laws of the land and have sometimes been punished for acting contrary to these laws.

- Some medical organizations are strongly influenced by religious teachings, which impose additional obligations on their members besides those applicable to all physicians.

- In many countries the organizations that set the standards for physician behaviour and monitor their compliance now have a significant non-physician membership.

The ethical directives of medical associations are general in nature; they cannot deal with every situation that physicians might face in their medical practice. In most situations, physicians have to decide for themselves what is the right way to act, but in making decisions, it is helpful to know what other physicians would do in similar situations. Medical codes of ethics and policy statements reflect a general consensus about the way physicians should act and they should be followed unless there are good reasons for acting otherwise.

> "...in making decisions, it is helpful to know what other physicians would do in similar situations."

## DOES MEDICAL ETHICS CHANGE?

There can be little doubt that some aspects of medical ethics have changed over the years. Until recently physicians had the right and the duty to decide how patients should be treated and there was no obligation to obtain the patient's informed consent. In contrast, the 1995 version of the WMA **Declaration on the Rights of the Patient** begins with this statement: "The relationship between physicians, their patients and broader society has undergone significant changes in recent times. While a physician should always act according to his/her conscience, and always in the best interests of the patient, equal effort must be made to guarantee patient autonomy and justice." Many individuals now consider that they are their own primary health providers and that the role of physicians is to act as their consultants or instructors. Although this emphasis on self-care is far from universal, it does seem to be spreading and is symptomatic of a more general evolution in the patient-physician relationship that gives rise to different ethical obligations for physicians than previously.

Until recently, physicians generally considered themselves *accountable* only to themselves, to their colleagues in the medical profession and, for religious believers, to God. Nowadays, they have additional accountabilities – to their patients, to third parties such as hospitals and *managed healthcare* organizations, to medical licensing and regulatory authorities, and often to courts of law. These different accountabilities can conflict with one

> "...different accountabilities can conflict with one another"

another, as will be evident in the discussion of dual loyalty in Chapter Three.

Medical ethics has changed in other ways. Participation in abortion was forbidden in medical codes of ethics until recently but now is tolerated under certain conditions by the medical profession in many countries. Whereas in traditional medical ethics the sole responsibility of physicians was to their individual patients, nowadays it is generally agreed that physicians should also consider the needs of society, for example, in allocating scarce healthcare resources (cf. Chapter Three).

Advances in medical science and technology raise new ethical issues that cannot be answered by traditional medical ethics. Assisted reproduction, genetics, health informatics and life-extending and enhancing technologies, all of which require the participation of physicians, have great potential for benefiting patients but also potential for harm depending on how they are put into practice. To help physicians decide whether and under what conditions they should participate in these activities, medical associations need to use different analytic methods than simply relying on existing codes of ethics.

Despite these obvious changes in medical ethics, there is widespread agreement among physicians that the fundamental values and ethical principles of medicine do not, or at least should not, change. Since it is inevitable that human beings will always be subject to illness, they will continue to have need of compassionate, competent and autonomous physicians to care for them.

## DOES MEDICAL ETHICS DIFFER FROM ONE COUNTRY TO ANOTHER?

Just as medical ethics can and does change over time, in response to developments in medical science and technology as well as in societal values, so does it vary from one country to another depending on these same factors. On euthanasia, for example, there is a significant difference of opinion among national medical associations. Some associations condemn it but others are neutral and at least one, the Royal Dutch Medical Association, accepts it under certain conditions. Likewise, regarding access to healthcare, some national associations support the equality of all citizens whereas others are willing to tolerate great inequalities. In some countries there is considerable interest in the ethical issues posed by advanced medical technology whereas in countries that do not have access to such technology, these ethical issues do not arise. Physicians in some countries are confident that they will not be forced by their government to do anything unethical while in other countries it may be difficult for them to meet their ethical obligations, for example, to maintain the confidentiality of patients in the face of police or army requirements to report 'suspicious' injuries.

Although these differences may seem significant, the similarities are far greater. Physicians throughout the world have much in common, and when they come together in organizations such as the WMA, they usually achieve agreement on controversial ethical issues, though this often requires lengthy debate. The fundamental values of medical ethics, such as compassion, competence and autonomy, along with physicians' experience and skills in all aspects of medicine and healthcare, provide a sound basis for analysing ethical issues in medicine and arriving at solutions that are in the best interests of individual patients and citizens and public health in general.

## THE ROLE OF THE WMA

As the only international organization that seeks to represent all physicians, regardless of nationality or specialty, the WMA has undertaken the role of establishing general standards in medical ethics that are applicable worldwide. From its beginning in 1947 it has worked to prevent any recurrence of the unethical conduct exhibited by physicians in Nazi Germany and elsewhere. The WMA's first task was to update the Hippocratic Oath for 20th century use; the result was the **Declaration of Geneva**, adopted at the WMA's 2nd General Assembly in 1948. It has been revised several times since, most recently in 1994. The second task was the development of an **International Code of Medical Ethics**, which was adopted at the 3rd General Assembly in 1949 and revised in 1968 and 1983. This code is currently undergoing further revision. The next task was to develop ethical guidelines for research on human subjects. This took much longer than the first two documents; it was not until 1964 that the guidelines were adopted as the **Declaration of Helsinki**. This document has also undergone periodic revision, most recently in 2000.

In addition to these foundational ethical statements, the WMA has adopted policy statements on more than 100 specific issues, the majority of which are ethical in nature while others deal with socio-medical topics, including medical education and health systems. Each year the WMA General Assembly revises some existing policies and/or adopts new ones.

> "...the WMA has undertaken the role of establishing general standards in medical ethics that are applicable worldwide."

## HOW DOES THE WMA DECIDE WHAT IS ETHICAL?

Achieving international agreement on controversial ethical issues is not an easy task, even within a relatively cohesive group such as physicians. The WMA ensures that its ethical policy statements reflect a consensus by requiring a 75% vote in favour of any new or revised policy at its annual Assembly. A precondition for achieving this degree of agreement is widespread consultation on draft

> "Achieving international agreement on controversial ethical issues is not an easy task"

statements, careful consideration of the comments received by the WMA Medical Ethics Committee and sometimes by a specially appointed workgroup on the issue, redrafting of the statement and often further consultation. The process can be lengthy, depending on the complexity and/or the novelty of the issue. For example, the most recent revision of the **Declaration of Helsinki** was begun early in 1997 and completed only in October 2000. Even then, outstanding issues remained and these continued to be studied by the Medical Ethics Committee and successive workgroups.

A good process is essential to, but does not guarantee, a good outcome. In deciding what is ethical, the WMA draws upon a long tradition of medical ethics as reflected in its previous ethical statements. It also takes note of other positions on the topic under consideration, both of national and international organizations and of individuals with skill in ethics. On some issues, such as informed consent, the WMA finds itself in agreement with the majority view. On others, such as the confidentiality of personal medical information, the position of physicians may have to be promoted forcefully against those of governments, health system administrators and/or commercial enterprises. A defining feature of the WMA's approach to ethics is the priority that it assigns to

> "On some issues, ... the position of physicians may have to be promoted forcefully against those of governments, health system administrators and/or commercial enterprises."

the individual patient or research subject. In reciting the **Declaration of Geneva**, the physician promises, "The health of my patient will be my first consideration." And the **Declaration of Helsinki** states, "In medical research on human subjects, considerations related to the well-being of the human subject should take precedence over the interests of science and society."

## HOW DO INDIVIDUALS DECIDE WHAT IS ETHICAL?

For individual physicians and medical students, medical ethics does not consist simply in following the recommendations of the WMA or other medical organizations. These recommendations are usually general in nature and individuals need to determine whether or not they apply to the situation at hand. Moreover, many ethical issues arise in medical practice for which there is no guidance from medical associations. Individuals

> "Individuals are ultimately responsible for making their own ethical decisions and for implementing them."

are ultimately responsible for making their own ethical decisions and for implementing them.

There are different ways of approaching ethical issues such as the ones in the cases at the beginning of this Manual. These can be divided roughly into two categories: non-rational and *rational*. It is important to note that non-rational does not mean irrational but simply that it is to be distinguished from the systematic, reflective use of reason in decision-making.

**Non-rational approaches:**

- **Obedience** is a common way of making ethical decisions, especially by children and those who work within authoritarian structures (e.g., the military, police, some religious organizations, many businesses). Morality consists in following the rules or instructions of those in authority, whether or not you agree with them.

- **Imitation** is similar to obedience in that it subordinates one's judgement about right and wrong to that of another person, in this case, a role model. Morality consists in following the example of the role model. This has been perhaps the most common way of learning medical ethics by aspiring physicians, with the role models being the senior consultants and the mode of moral learning being observation and assimilation of the values portrayed.

- **Feeling** or **desire** is a subjective approach to moral decision-making and behaviour. What is right is what feels right or satisfies one's desire; what is wrong is what feels wrong or frustrates one's desire. The measure of morality is to be found within each individual and, of course, can vary greatly from one individual to another, and even within the same individual over time.

- **Intuition** is an immediate perception of the right way to act in a situation. It is similar to desire in that it is entirely subjective; however, it differs because of its location in the mind rather than the will. To that extent it comes closer to the rational forms of ethical decision-making than do obedience, imitation, feeling and desire. However, it is neither systematic nor reflexive but directs moral decisions through a simple flash of insight. Like feeling and desire, it can vary greatly from one individual to another, and even within the same individual over time.

- **Habit** is a very efficient method of moral decision-making since there is no need to repeat a systematic decision-making process each time a moral issue arises similar to one that has been dealt with previously. However, there are bad habits (e.g., lying) as well as good ones (e.g., truth-telling); moreover, situations that appear similar may require significantly different decisions. As useful as habit is, therefore, one cannot place all one's confidence in it.

**Rational approaches:**

As the study of morality, ethics recognises the prevalence of these non-rational approaches to decision-making and behaviour. However, it is primarily concerned with rational approaches. Four such approaches are deontology, consequentialism, principlism and virtue ethics:

- **Deontology** involves a search for well-founded rules that can serve as the basis for making moral decisions. An example of such a rule is, "Treat all people as equals." Its foundation may be religious (for example, the belief that all God's human creatures are equal) or non-religious (for example, human beings share almost all of the same genes). Once the rules are established, they have to be applied in specific situations, and here there is often room for disagreement about what the rules require (for example, whether the rule against killing another human being would prohibit abortion or capital punishment).

- **Consequentialism** bases ethical decision-making on an analysis of the likely consequences or outcomes of different choices and actions. The right action is the one that produces the best outcomes. Of course there can be disagreement about what counts as a good outcome. One of the best-known forms of consequentialism, namely **utilitarianism**, uses 'utility' as its measure and defines this as 'the greatest good for the greatest number'. Other outcome measures used in healthcare decision-making include cost-effectiveness and quality of life as measured in QALYs (quality-adjusted life-years) or DALYs (disability-adjusted life-years). Supporters of consequentialism generally do not have much use for principles; they are too difficult to identify, prioritise and apply, and in any case they do not take into account what in their view really matters in moral decision-making, i.e., the outcomes. However, this setting aside of principles leaves consequentialism open to the charge that it accepts that 'the end justifies the means', for example, that individual human rights can be sacrificed to attain a social goal.

- **Principlism**, as its name implies, uses ethical principles as the basis for making moral decisions. It applies these principles to particular cases or situations in order to determine what is the right thing to do, taking into account both rules and consequences. Principlism has been extremely influential in recent ethical debates, especially in the USA. Four principles in particular, respect for autonomy, *beneficence*, *non-maleficence* and *justice*, have been identified as the most important for ethical decision-making in medical practice. Principles do indeed play an important role in rational decision-making. However, the choice of these four principles, and especially the prioritisation of respect for autonomy over the others, is a reflection of Western liberal culture and is not necessarily universal. Moreover, these four principles often clash in particular situations and there is need for some criteria or process for resolving such conflicts.

- **Virtue ethics** focuses less on decision-making and more on the character of decision-makers as reflected in their behaviour. A virtue is a type of moral excellence. As noted above, one virtue that is especially important for physicians is compassion. Others include honesty, prudence and dedication. Physicians who possess these virtues are more likely to make good decisions and to implement them in a good way. However, even virtuous individuals often are unsure how to act in particular situations and are not immune from making wrong decisions.

None of these four approaches, or others that have been proposed, has been able to win universal assent. Individuals differ among themselves in their preference for a rational approach to ethical decision-making just as they do in their preference for a non-rational approach. This can be explained partly by the fact that each approach has both strengths and weaknesses. Perhaps a combination of all four approaches that includes the best features of each is the best way to make ethical decisions rationally. It would take serious account of rules and principles by identifying the ones most relevant to the situation or case at hand and by attempting to implement them to the greatest extent possible. It would also examine the likely consequences of alternative decisions and determine which consequences would be preferable. Finally, it would attempt to ensure that the behaviour of the decision-maker both in coming to a decision and in implementing it is admirable. Such a process could comprise the following steps:

1. Determine whether the issue at hand is an ethical one.

2. Consult authoritative sources such as medical association codes of ethics and policies and respected colleagues to see how physicians generally deal with such issues.

3. Consider alternative solutions in light of the principles and values they uphold and their likely consequences.

4. Discuss your proposed solution with those whom it will affect.

5. Make your decision and act on it, with sensitivity to others affected.

6. Evaluate your decision and be prepared to act differently in future.

# CONCLUSION

This chapter sets the stage for what follows. When dealing with specific issues in medical ethics, it is good to keep in mind that physicians have faced many of the same issues throughout history and that their accumulated experience and wisdom can be very valuable today. The WMA and other medical organizations carry on this tradition and provide much helpful ethical guidance to physicians. However, despite a large measure of consensus among physicians on ethical issues, individuals can and do disagree on how to deal with specific cases. Moreover, the views of physicians can be quite different from those of patients and of other healthcare providers. As a first step in resolving ethical conflicts, it is important for physicians to understand different approaches to ethical decision-making, including their own and those of the people with whom they are interacting. This will help them determine for themselves the best way to act and to explain their decisions to others.

... ethica

ethica médica

medisinsk etikk

medical ethics

Læknisfræðileg siðfræði

Medyczna etyka

倫理の倫理

רפואה אתיקה

medisinsk etikk

medica

medizinische Ethik

lääketieteen etiikka

# CHAPTER TWO – PHYSICIANS AND PATIENTS

Compassionate doctor
© Jose Luis Pelaez, Inc./CORBIS

## OBJECTIVES

After working through this chapter you should be able to:

· explain why all patients are deserving of respect and equal treatment;

· identify the essential elements of informed consent;

· explain how medical decisions should be made for patients who are incapable of making their own decisions;

· explain the justification for patient confidentiality and recognise legitimate exceptions to confidentiality;

· recognize the principal ethical issues that occur at the beginning and end of life;

· summarize the arguments for and against the practice of euthanasia/assisted suicide and the difference between these actions and *palliative care* or forgoing treatment.

## CASE STUDY #1

Dr. P, an experienced and skilled surgeon, is about to finish night duty at a medium-sized community hospital. A young woman is brought to the hospital by her mother, who leaves immediately after telling the intake nurse that she has to look after her other children. The patient is bleeding vaginally and is in a great deal of pain. Dr. P examines her and decides that she has had either a miscarriage or a self-induced abortion. He does a quick dilatation and curettage and tells the nurse to ask the patient whether she can afford to stay in the hospital until it is safe for her to be discharged. Dr. Q comes in to replace Dr. P, who goes home without having spoken to the patient.

### WHAT'S SPECIAL ABOUT THE PHYSICIAN-PATIENT RELATIONSHIP?

The physician-patient relationship is the cornerstone of medical practice and therefore of medical ethics. As noted above, the **Declaration of Geneva** requires of the physician that "The health of my patient will be my first consideration," and the **International Code of Medical Ethics** states, "A physician shall owe his patients complete loyalty and all the resources of his science." As discussed in Chapter One, the traditional interpretation of the physician-patient relationship as a paternalistic one, in which the physician made the decisions and the patient submitted to them, has been widely rejected in recent years, both in ethics and in law. Since many patients are either unable or unwilling to make decisions about their medical care, however, patient autonomy is often very problematic.

Equally problematic are other aspects of the relationship, such as the physician's obligation to maintain patient confidentiality in an era of computerized medical records and managed care, and the duty to preserve life in the face of requests to hasten death.

This section will deal with six topics that pose particularly vexing problems to physicians in their daily practice: respect and equal treatment; communication and consent; decision-making for incompetent patients; confidentiality; beginning-of-life issues; and end-of-life issues.

> **"The health of my patient will be my first consideration"**

## RESPECT AND EQUAL TREATMENT

The belief that all human beings deserve respect and equal treatment is relatively recent. In most societies disrespectful and unequal treatment of individuals and groups was accepted as normal and natural. Slavery was one such practice that was not eradicated in the European colonies and the USA until the 19th century and still exists in some parts of the world. The end of institutional discrimination against non-whites in countries such as South Africa is much more recent. Women still experience lack of respect and unequal treatment in most countries. Discrimination on the basis of age, disability or sexual orientation is widespread. Clearly, there remains considerable resistance to the claim that all people should be treated as equals.

The gradual and still ongoing conversion of humanity to a belief in human equality began in the 17th and 18th centuries in Europe and North America. It was led by two opposed ideologies: a new interpretation of Christian faith and an anti-Christian rationalism. The former inspired the American Revolution and Bill of Rights; the latter, the French Revolution and related political developments.

Under these two influences, democracy very gradually took hold and began to spread throughout the world. It was based on a belief in the political equality of all men (and, much later, women) and the consequent right to have a say in who should govern them.

In the 20th century there was considerable elaboration of the concept of human equality in terms of human rights. One of the first acts of the newly established United Nations was to develop the **Universal Declaration of Human Rights** (1948), which states in article 1, "All human beings are born free and equal in dignity and rights." Many other international and national bodies have produced statements of rights, either for all human beings, for all citizens in a specific country, or for certain groups of individuals ('children's rights', 'patients' rights', 'consumers' rights', etc.). Numerous organizations have been formed to promote action on these statements. Unfortunately, though, human rights are still not respected in many countries.

The medical profession has had somewhat conflicting views on patient equality and rights over the years. On the one hand, physicians have been told not to "permit considerations of age, disease or disability, creed, ethnic origin, gender, nationality, political affiliation, race, sexual orientation, or social standing to intervene between my duty and my patient" (**Declaration of Geneva**). At the same time physicians have claimed the right to refuse to accept a patient, except in an emergency. Although the legitimate grounds for such refusal include a full practice, (lack of) educational qualifications and specialization, if physicians do not have to give any reason for refusing a patient, they can easily practise discrimination without being held accountable. A physician's conscience, rather than the law or disciplinary authorities, may be the only means of preventing abuses of human rights in this regard.

Even if physicians do not offend against respect and human equality in their choice of patients, they can still do so in their attitudes towards and treatment of patients. The case study described at the beginning of this chapter illustrates this problem. As noted in Chapter One, compassion is one of the core values of medicine and is an essential element of a good therapeutic relationship. Compassion is based on respect for the patient's dignity and values but goes further in acknowledging and responding to the patient's vulnerability in the face of illness and/or disability. If patients sense the physician's compassion, they will be more likely to trust the physician to act in their best interests, and this trust can contribute to the healing process.

The trust that is essential to the physician-patient relationship has generally been interpreted to mean that physicians should not desert patients whose care they have undertaken. The WMA's **International Code of Medical Ethics** implies that the only reason for ending a physician-patient relationship is if the patient requires another physician with different skills: "A physician shall owe his patients complete loyalty and all the resources of his science. Whenever an examination or treatment is beyond the physician's capacity he should summon another physician who has the necessary ability." However, there are many other reasons for a physician wanting to terminate a relationship with a patient, for example, the physician's moving or stopping practice, the patient's refusal or inability to pay for the physician's services, dislike of the patient and the physician for each other, the patient's refusal to comply with the physician's recommendations, etc. The reasons may be entirely legitimate, or they may be unethical. When considering such an action, physicians should consult their Code of Ethics and other relevant guidance

> "…in ending a physician-patient relationship… physicians… should be prepared to justify their decision, to themselves, to the patient and to a third party if appropriate."

documents and carefully examine their motives. They should be prepared to justify their decision, to themselves, to the patient and to a third party if appropriate. If the motive is legitimate, the physician should help the patient find another suitable physician or, if this is not possible, should give the patient adequate notice of withdrawal of services so that the patient can find alternative medical care. If the motive is not legitimate, for example, racial prejudice, the physician should take steps to deal with this defect.

Many physicians, especially those in the public sector, often have no choice of the patients they treat. Some patients are violent and pose a threat to the physician's safety. Others can only be described as obnoxious because of their antisocial attitudes and behaviour. Have such patients forsaken their right to respect and equal treatment, or are physicians expected to make extra, perhaps even heroic, efforts to establish and maintain therapeutic relationships with them? With such patients, physicians must balance their responsibility for their own safety and well-being and that of their staff with their duty to promote the well-being of the patients. They should attempt to find ways to honour both of these obligations. If this is not possible, they should try to make alternative arrangements for the care of the patients.

Another challenge to the principle of respect and equal treatment for all patients arises in the care of infectious patients. The focus here is often on HIV/AIDS, not only because it is a life-threatening disease but also because it is often associated with social prejudices. However, there are many other serious infections including some that are more easily transmissible to healthcare workers than HIV/AIDS. Some physicians hesitate to perform invasive procedures on patients with such conditions because of the possibility that they, the physicians, might become infected. However, medical codes of ethics make no exception for infectious patients with regard to the physician's duty to treat all patients equally. The WMA's **Statement**

**on the Professional Responsibility of Physicians in Treating AIDS Patients** puts it this way:

> AIDS patients are entitled to competent medical care with compassion and respect for human dignity.

> A physician may not ethically refuse to treat a patient whose condition is within the physician's current realm of competence, solely because the patient is seropositive.

> "A person who is afflicted with AIDS needs competent, compassionate treatment."

> Medical ethics do not permit categorical discrimination against a patient based solely on his or her seropositivity. A person who is afflicted with AIDS needs competent, compassionate treatment. A physician who is not able to provide the care and services required by persons with AIDS should make an appropriate referral to those physicians or facilities that are equipped to provide such services. Until the referral can be accomplished, the physician must care for the patient to the best of his or her ability.

The intimate nature of the physician-patient relationship can give rise to sexual attraction. A fundamental rule of traditional medical ethics is that such attraction must be resisted. The Oath of Hippocrates includes the following promise: "Whatever houses I may visit, I will come for the benefit of the sick, remaining free of all intentional injustice, of all mischief and in particular of sexual relations with both female and male persons...." In recent years many medical association have restated this prohibition of sexual relations between physicians and their patients. The reasons for this are as valid today as they were in Hippocrates' time, 2500 years ago. Patients are vulnerable and put their trust in physicians to treat them well. They may feel unable to resist sexual advances of physicians for fear that their treatment will be jeopardized. Moreover, the clinical judgment of a physician can be adversely affected by emotional involvement with a patient.

This latter reason applies as well to physicians treating their family members, which is strongly discouraged in many medical codes of ethics. However, as with some other statements in codes of ethics, its application can vary according to circumstances. For example, solo practitioners working in remote areas may have to provide medical care for their family members, especially in emergency situations.

## COMMUNICATION AND CONSENT

Informed consent is one of the central concepts of present-day medical ethics. The right of patients to make decisions about their healthcare has been enshrined in legal and ethical statements throughout the world. The WMA **Declaration on the Rights of the Patient** states:

> The patient has the right to self-determination, to make free decisions regarding himself/herself. The physician will inform the patient of the consequences of his/her decisions. A mentally competent adult patient has the right to give or withhold consent to any diagnostic procedure or therapy. The patient has the right to the information necessary to make his/her decisions. The patient should understand clearly what is the purpose of any test or treatment, what the results would imply, and what would be the implications of withholding consent.

A necessary condition for informed consent is good communication between physician and patient. When medical paternalism was normal, communication was relatively simple; it consisted of the physician's orders to the patient to comply with such and such a treatment. Nowadays communication requires much more of physicians. They must provide patients with all the information they need to make their decisions. This involves explaining complex medical diagnoses, prognoses and treatment regimes in simple language, ensuring that patients understand the treatment options, including the advantages and disadvantages of each, answering any questions they may have, and understanding whatever decision the patient has reached and, if possible, the reasons for it. Good communication skills do not come naturally to most people; they must be developed and maintained with conscious effort and periodic review.

Two major obstacles to good physician-patient communication are differences of language and culture. If the physician and the patient do not speak the same language, an interpreter will be required. Unfortunately, in many settings there are no qualified interpreters and the physician must seek out the best available person for the task. Culture, which includes but is much broader than language, raises additional communication issues. Because of different cultural understandings of the nature and causes of illness, patients may not understand the diagnosis and treatment options provided by their physician. In such circumstances physicians should make every reasonable effort to probe their patients' understanding of health and healing and communicate their recommendations to the patients as best they can.

If the physician has successfully communicated to the patient all the information the patient needs and wants to know about his or her diagnosis, prognosis and treatment options, the patient will then be in a position to make an informed decision about how to proceed. Although the term 'consent' implies acceptance of treatment, the concept of informed consent applies equally to refusal of treatment or to choice among alternative treatments. Competent patients have

> "Competent patients have the right to refuse treatment, even when the refusal will result in disability or death."

the right to refuse treatment, even when the refusal will result in disability or death.

Evidence of consent can be explicit or implicit (implied). Explicit consent is given orally or in writing. Consent is implied when the patient indicates a willingness to undergo a certain procedure or treatment by his or her behaviour. For example, consent for venipuncture is implied by the action of presenting one's arm. For treatments that entail risk or involve more than mild discomfort, it is preferable to obtain explicit rather than implied consent.

There are two exceptions to the requirement for informed consent by competent patients:

- Situations where patients voluntarily give over their decision-making authority to the physician or to a third party. Because of the complexity of the matter or because the patient has complete confidence in the physician's judgement, the patient may tell the physician, "Do what you think is best." Physicians should not be eager to act on such requests but should provide patients with basic information about the treatment options and encourage them to make their own decisions. However, if after such encouragement the patient still wants the physician to decide, the physician should do so according to the best interests of the patient.

- Instances where the disclosure of information would cause harm to the patient. The traditional concept of 'therapeutic privilege' is invoked in such cases; it allows physicians to withhold medical information if disclosure would be likely to result in serious physical, psychological or emotional harm to the patient, for example, if the patient would be likely to commit suicide if the diagnosis indicates a terminal illness. This privilege is open to great abuse, and physicians should make use of it only in extreme circumstances. They should start with the expectation that all patients are able to cope with the facts and reserve nondisclosure for cases in which they are convinced that more harm will result from telling the truth than from not telling it.

In some cultures, it is widely held that the physician's obligation to provide information to the patient does not apply when the diagnosis is a terminal illness. It is felt that such information would cause the patient to despair and would make the remaining days of life much more miserable than if there were hope of recovery. Throughout the world it is not uncommon for family members of patients to plead with physicians not to tell the patients that they are dying. Physicians do have to be sensitive to cultural as well as personal factors when communicating bad news, especially of impending death. Nevertheless, the patient's right to informed consent is becoming more and more widely accepted, and the physician has a primary duty to help patients exercise this right.

In keeping with the growing trend towards considering healthcare as a consumer product and patients as consumers, patients and their families not infrequently demand access to medical services that, in the considered opinion of physicians, are not appropriate. Examples of such services range from antibiotics for viral conditions to intensive care for brain-dead patients to promising but unproven drugs or surgical procedures. Some patients claim a 'right' to any medical service that they feel can benefit them, and often physicians are only too willing to oblige, even when they are convinced that the service can offer no medical benefit for the patient's condition. This problem is especially serious in situations where resources are limited and providing 'futile' or 'nonbeneficial' treatments to some patients means that other patients are left untreated.

**Futile** and **nonbeneficial** can be understood as follows. In some situations a physician can determine that a treatment is 'medically' futile or nonbeneficial because it offers no reasonable hope of recovery or improvement or because the patient is permanently unable to experience any benefit. In other cases the utility and benefit of a treatment can only be determined with reference to the patient's subjective judgement about his or her overall well-being.

As a general rule a patient should be involved in determining futility in his or her case. In exceptional circumstances such discussions may not be in the patient's best interests. The physician has no obligation to offer a patient futile or nonbeneficial treatment.

> "The physician has no obligation to offer a patient futile or nonbeneficial treatment."

The principle of informed consent incorporates the patient's right to choose from among the options presented by the physician. To what extent patients and their families have a right to services not recommended by physicians is becoming a major topic of controversy in ethics, law and public policy. Until this matter is decided by governments, medical insurance providers and/or professional organisations, individual physicians will have to decide for themselves whether they should accede to requests for inappropriate treatments. They should refuse such requests if they are convinced that the treatment would produce more harm than benefit. They should also feel free to refuse if the treatment

> Do patients have a right to services not recommended by physicians?

is unlikely to be beneficial, even if it is not harmful, although the possibility of a placebo effect should not be discounted. If limited resources are an issue, they should bring this to the attention of whoever is responsible for allocating resources.

# DECISION-MAKING FOR INCOMPETENT PATIENTS

Many patients are not competent to make decisions for themselves. Examples include young children, individuals affected by certain psychiatric or neurological conditions, and those who are temporarily unconscious or comatose. These patients require substitute decision-makers, either the physician or another person. Ethical issues arise in the determination of the appropriate substitute decision-maker and in the choice of criteria for decisions on behalf of incompetent patients.

When medical paternalism prevailed, the physician was considered to be the appropriate decision-maker for incompetent patients. Physicians might consult with family members about treatment options, but the final decisions were theirs to make. Physicians have been gradually losing this authority in many countries as patients are given the opportunity to name their own substitute decision-makers to act for them when they become incompetent. In addition, some states specify the appropriate substitute decision-makers in descending order (e.g., husband or wife, adult children, brothers and sisters, etc.). In such cases physicians make decisions for patients only when the designated substitute cannot be found, as often happens in emergency situations. The WMA **Declaration on the Rights of the Patient** states the physician's duty in this matter as follows:

> If the patient is unconscious or otherwise unable to express his/her will, informed consent must be obtained, whenever possible, from a legally entitled representative where legally relevant. If a legally entitled representative is not available, but a medical intervention is urgently needed, consent of the patient may be presumed, unless it is obvious and beyond any doubt on the basis of the patient's previous firm

expression or conviction that he/she would refuse consent to the intervention in that situation.

Problems arise when those claiming to be the appropriate substitute decision-makers, for example different family members, do not agree among themselves or when they do agree, their decision is, in the physician's opinion, not in the patient's best interests. In the first instance the physician can serve a mediating function, but if the disagreement persists, it can be resolved in other ways, for example, by letting the senior member of the family decide or by voting. In cases of serious disagreement between the substitute decision-maker and the physician, the **Declaration on the Rights of the Patient** offers the following advice: "If the patient's legally entitled representative, or a person authorized by the patient, forbids treatment which is, in the opinion of the physician, in the patient's best interest, the physician should challenge this decision in the relevant legal or other institution."

The principles and procedures for informed consent that were discussed in the previous section are just as applicable to substitute decision-making as to patients making their own decisions. Physicians have the same duty to provide all the information the substitute decision-makers need to make their decisions. This involves explaining complex medical diagnoses, prognoses and treatment regimes in simple language, ensuring that the decision-makers understand the treatment options, including the advantages and disadvantages of each, answering any questions they may have, and understanding whatever decision they reach and, if possible, the reasons for it.

The principal criteria to be used for treatment decisions for an incompetent patient are his or her preferences, if these are known. The preferences may be found in an *advance directive* or may have been communicated to the designated substitute decision-maker, the physician or other members of the healthcare team. When an incompetent patient's preferences are not known, treatment decisions should be based on the patient's best interests, taking into account: (a) the patient's diagnosis and prognosis; (b) the patient's known values; (c) information received from those who are significant in the patient's life and who could help in determining his or her best interests; and (d) aspects of the patient's culture and religion that would influence a treatment decision. This approach is less certain than if the patient has left specific instructions about treatment, but it does enable the substitute decision-maker to infer, in light of other choices the patient has made and his or her approach to life in general, what he or she would decide in the present situation.

Competence to make medical decisions can be difficult to assess, especially in young people and those whose capacity for reasoning has been impaired by acute or chronic illness. A person may be competent to make decisions regarding some aspects of life but not others; as well, competence can be intermittent -- a person may be lucid and oriented at certain times of the day and not at others. Although such patients may not be legally competent, their preferences should be taken into account when decisions are being made for them. The **Declaration on the Rights of the Patient** states the matter thus: "If a patient is a minor or otherwise legally incompetent, the consent of a legally entitled representative, where legally relevant, is required. Nevertheless the patient must be involved in the decision-making to the fullest extent allowed by his/her capacity."

> "...the patient must be involved in the decision-making to the fullest extent allowed by his/her capacity"

Not infrequently, patients are unable to make a reasoned, well thought-out decision regarding different treatment options due to the discomfort and distraction caused by their disease. However, they may still be able to indicate their rejection of a specific intervention, an intravenous feeding tube, for example. In such cases, these expressions of dissent should be taken very seriously, although they need to be considered in light of the overall goals of their treatment plan.

Patients suffering from psychiatric or neurological disorders who are judged to pose a danger to themselves or to others raise particularly difficult ethical issues. It is important to honour their human rights, especially the right to freedom, to the greatest extent possible. Nevertheless, they may have to be confined and/or treated against their will in order to prevent harm to themselves or others. A distinction can be made between involuntary confinement and involuntary treatment. Some patient advocates defend the right of these individuals to refuse treatment even if they have to be confined as a result. A legitimate reason for refusing treatment could be painful experience with treatments in the past, for example, the severe side effects of psychotropic medications. When serving as substitute decision-makers for such patients, physicians should ensure that the patients really do pose a danger, and not just an annoyance, to others or to themselves. They should try to ascertain the patients' preferences regarding treatment, and the reasons for these preferences, even if in the end the preferences cannot be fulfilled.

## CONFIDENTIALITY

The physician's duty to keep patient information confidential has been a cornerstone of medical ethics since the time of Hippocrates. The Hippocratic Oath states: "What I may see or hear in the course

> "A physician shall preserve absolute confidentiality on all he knows about his patient even after the patient has died."

of the treatment or even outside of the treatment in regard to the life of men, which on no account one must spread abroad, I will keep to myself holding such things shameful to be spoken about." The Oath, and some more recent versions, allow no exception to this duty of confidentiality. For example, the WMA's **International Code of Medical Ethics** requires that "A physician shall preserve absolute confidentiality on all he knows about his patient even after the patient has died." However, other codes reject this absolutist approach to confidentiality. The possibility that breaches of confidentiality are sometimes justified calls for clarification of the very idea of confidentiality.

The high value that is placed on confidentiality has three sources: autonomy, respect for others and trust. Autonomy relates to confidentiality in that personal information about an individual belongs to him or her and should not be made known to others without his or her consent. When an individual reveals personal information to another, a physician or nurse for example, or when information comes to light through a medical test, those in the know are bound to keep it confidential unless authorized to divulge it by the individual concerned.

Confidentiality is also important because human beings deserve respect. One important way of showing them respect is by preserving their privacy. In the medical setting, privacy is often greatly compromised, but this is all the more reason to prevent further unnecessary intrusions into a person's private life. Since individuals differ regarding their desire for privacy, we cannot assume that everyone wants to be treated as we would want to be. Care must be taken to determine which personal information a patient wants to keep secret and which he or she is willing to have revealed to others.

Trust is an essential part of the physician-patient relationship. In order to receive medical care, patients have to reveal personal information to physicians and others who may be total strangers to them---information that they would not want anyone else to know. They must have good reason to trust their caregivers not to divulge this information. The basis of this trust is the ethical and legal standards of confidentiality that healthcare professionals are expected to uphold. Without an understanding that their disclosures will be kept secret, patients may withhold personal information. This can hinder physicians in their efforts to provide effective interventions or to attain certain public health goals.

The WMA **Declaration on the Rights of the Patient** summarises the patient's right to confidentiality as follows:

- All identifiable information about a patient's health status, medical condition, diagnosis, prognosis and treatment and all other information of a personal kind, must be kept confidential, even after death. Exceptionally, the patient's relatives may have a right of access to information that would inform them of their health risks.

- Confidential information can only be disclosed if the patient gives explicit consent or if expressly provided for in the law. Information can be disclosed to other healthcare providers only on a strictly "need to know" basis unless the patient has given explicit consent.

- All identifiable patient data must be protected. The protection of the data must be appropriate to the manner of its storage. Human substances from which identifiable data can be derived must be likewise protected.

As this WMA Declaration states, there are exceptions to the requirement to maintain confidentiality. Some of these are relatively non-problematic; others raise very difficult ethical issues for physicians.

Routine breaches of confidentiality occur frequently in most healthcare institutions. Many individuals – physicians, nurses, laboratory technicians, students, etc. – require access to a patient's health records in order to provide adequate care to that person and, for students, to learn how to practise medicine. Where patients speak a different language than their caregivers, there is a need for interpreters to facilitate communication. In cases of patients who are not competent to make their own medical decisions, other individuals have to be given information about them in order to make decisions on their behalf and to care for them. Physicians routinely inform the family members of a deceased person about the cause of death. These breaches of confidentiality are usually justified, but they should be kept to a minimum and those who gain access to confidential information should be made aware of the need not to spread it any further than is necessary for the patient's benefit. Where possible, patients should be informed that such breaches occur.

Another generally accepted reason for breaching confidentiality is to comply with legal requirements. For example, many jurisdictions have laws for the mandatory reporting of patients who suffer from designated diseases, those deemed not fit to drive and those suspected of child abuse. Physicians should be aware of the legal requirements for the disclosure

> "...physicians should view with a critical eye any legal requirement to breach confidentiality and assure themselves that it is justified before adhering to it."

of patient information where they work. However, legal requirements can conflict with the respect for human rights that underlies medical ethics. Therefore, physicians should view with a critical eye any legal requirement to breach confidentiality and assure themselves that it is justified before adhering to it.

If physicians are persuaded to comply with legal requirements to disclose their patients' medical information, it is desirable that they discuss with the patients the necessity of any disclosure before it occurs and enlist their co-operation. For example, it is preferable that a patient suspected of child abuse call the child protection authorities in the physician's presence to self-report, or that the physician obtain his or her consent before the authorities are notified. This approach will prepare the way for subsequent interventions. If such co-operation is not forthcoming and the physician has reason to believe any delay in notification may put a child at risk of serious harm, then the physician ought to immediately notify child protection authorities and subsequently inform the patient that this has been done.

In addition to those breaches of confidentiality that are required by law, physicians may have an ethical duty to impart confidential information to others who could be at risk of harm from the patient. Two situations in which this can occur are when a patient tells a psychiatrist that he intends to harm another person and when a physician is convinced that an HIV-positive patient is going to continue to have unprotected sexual intercourse with his spouse or other partners.

Conditions for breaching confidentiality when not required by law are that the expected harm is believed to be imminent, serious (and irreversible), unavoidable except by unauthorised disclosure, and greater than the harm likely to result from disclosure. In determining the proportionality of these respective harms, the physician needs to assess and compare the seriousness of the harms and the likelihood of their occurrence. In cases of doubt, it would be wise for the physician to seek expert advice.

When a physician has determined that the duty to warn justifies an unauthorised disclosure, two further decisions must be made. Whom should the physician tell? How much should be told? Generally speaking, the disclosure should contain only that information necessary to prevent the anticipated harm and should be directed only to those who need the information in order to prevent the harm. Reasonable steps should be taken to minimize the harm and offence to the patient that may arise from the disclosure. It is recommended that the physician should inform the patient that confidentiality might be breached for his or her own protection and that of any potential victim. The patient's co-operation should be enlisted if possible.

In the case of an HIV-positive patient, disclosure to a spouse or current sexual partner may not be unethical and, indeed, may be justified when the patient is unwilling to inform the person(s) at risk. Such disclosure requires that all of the following conditions are met: the partner is at risk of infection with HIV and has no other reasonable means of knowing the risk; the patient has refused to inform his or her sexual partner; the patient has refused an offer of assistance by the physician to do so on the patient's behalf; and the physician has informed the patient of his or her intention to disclose the information to the partner.

The medical care of suspected and convicted criminals poses particular difficulties with regard to confidentiality. Although physicians providing care to those in custody have limited independence, they should do their best to treat these patients as they would any others. In particular, they should safeguard confidentiality by not revealing details of the patient's medical condition to prison authorities without first obtaining the patient's consent.

# BEGINNING-OF-LIFE ISSUES

Many of the most prominent issues in medical ethics relate to the beginning of human life. The limited scope of this Manual means that these issues cannot be treated in detail here but it is worth listing them so that they can be recognized as ethical in nature and dealt with as such. Each of them has been the subject of extensive analysis by medical associations, ethicists and government advisory bodies, and in many countries there are laws, regulations and policies dealing with them.

- **CONTRACEPTION** – although there is increasing international recognition of a woman's right to control her fertility, including the prevention of unwanted pregnancies, physicians still have to deal with difficult issues such as requests for contraceptives from minors and explaining the risks of different methods of contraception.

- **ASSISTED REPRODUCTION** – for couples (and individuals) who cannot conceive naturally there are various techniques of assisted reproduction, such as artificial insemination and in-vitro fertilization and embryo transfer, widely available in major medical centres. *Surrogate or substitute gestation* is another alternative. None of these techniques is unproblematic, either in individual cases or for public policies.

- **PRENATAL GENETIC SCREENING** – genetic tests are now available for determining whether an embryo or foetus is affected by certain genetic abnormalities and whether it is male or female. Depending on the findings, a decision can be made whether or not to proceed with pregnancy. Physicians need to determine when to offer such tests and how to explain the results to patients.

- **ABORTION** – this has long been one of the most divisive issues in medical ethics, both for physicians and for public authorities. The WMA **Statement on Therapeutic Abortion** acknowledges this diversity of opinion and belief and concludes that "This is a matter of individual conviction and conscience which must be respected."

- **SEVERELY COMPROMISED NEONATES** – because of extreme prematurity or congenital abnormalities, some neonates have a very poor prognosis for survival. Difficult decisions often have to be made whether to attempt to prolong their lives or allow them to die.

- **RESEARCH ISSUES** – these include the production of new embryos or the use of 'spare' embryos (those not wanted for reproductive purposes) to obtain stem cells for potential therapeutic applications, testing of new techniques for assisted reproduction, and experimentation on foetuses.

## END-OF-LIFE ISSUES

End-of-life issues range from attempts to prolong the lives of dying patients through highly experimental technologies, such as the implantation of animal organs, to efforts to terminate life prematurely through euthanasia and medically assisted suicide. In between these extremes lie numerous issues regarding the initiation or withdrawing of potentially life-extending treatments, the care of terminally ill patients and the advisability and use of advance directives.

Two issues deserve particular attention: euthanasia and assistance in suicide.

- **EUTHANASIA** means knowingly and intentionally performing an act that is clearly intended to end another person's life and that includes the following elements: the subject is a competent,

decisions about when to initiate these treatments and when to withdraw them if they are not working.

As discussed above in relation to communication and consent, competent patients have the right to refuse any medical treatment, even if the refusal results in their death. Individuals differ greatly with regard to their attitude towards dying; some will do anything to prolong their lives, no matter how much pain and suffering it involves, while others so look forward to dying that they refuse even simple measures that are likely to keep them alive, such as antibiotics for bacterial pneumonia. Once physicians have made every effort to provide patients with information about the available treatments and their likelihood of success, they must respect the patients' decisions about the initiation or continuation of any treatment.

End-of-life decision-making for incompetent patients presents greater difficulties. If patients have clearly expressed their wishes in advance, for example in an advance directive, the decision will be easier, although such directives are often very vague and need to be interpreted with respect to the patient's actual condition. If patients have not adequately expressed their wishes, the appropriate substitute decision-maker must use another criterion for treatment decisions, namely, the best interests of the patient.

# BACK TO THE CASE STUDY

According to the analysis of the physician-patient relationship presented in this chapter, Dr. P's conduct was deficient in several respects: (1) COMMUNICATION – he made no attempt to communicate with the patient regarding the cause of her condition, treatment options or her ability to afford to stay in the hospital while she recovered; (2) CONSENT – he did not obtain her informed consent to treatment: (3) COMPASSION – his dealings with her displayed little compassion for her plight. His surgical treatment may have been highly competent and he may have been tired at the end of a long shift, but that does not excuse the breaches of ethics.

# CHAPTER THREE – PHYSICIANS AND SOCIETY

**Looking AIDS in the Face**
© Gideon Mendel/CORBIS

## OBJECTIVES

After working through this chapter you should be able to:

· recognize conflicts between the physician's obligations to patients and to society and identify the reasons for the conflicts

· identify and deal with the ethical issues involved in allocating scarce medical resources

· recognize physician responsibilities for public and global health.

## CASE STUDY #2

Dr. S is becoming increasingly frustrated with patients who come to her either before or after consulting another health practitioner for the same ailment. She considers this to be a waste of health resources as well as counter-productive for the health of the patients. She decides to tell these patients that she will no longer treat them if they continue to see other practitioners for the same ailment. She intends to approach her national medical association to lobby the government to prevent this form of misallocation of healthcare resources.

### WHAT'S SPECIAL ABOUT THE PHYSICIAN-SOCIETY RELATIONSHIP?

Medicine is a profession. The term 'profession' has two distinct, although closely related, meanings: (1) an occupation that is characterized by dedication to the well-being of others, high moral standards, a body of knowledge and skills, and a high level of autonomy; and (2) all the individuals who practise that occupation. 'The medical profession' can mean either the practice of medicine or physicians in general.

Medical professionalism involves not just the relationship between a physician and a patient, as discussed in Chapter Two, and relationships with colleagues and other health professionals, which will be treated in Chapter Four. It also involves a relationship with society. This relationship can be characterized as a 'social contract' whereby society grants the profession privileges, including exclusive or primary responsibility for the provision of certain services and a high degree of self-regulation, and in return, the profession agrees to use these privileges primarily for the benefit of others and only secondarily for its own benefit.

Medicine is today, more than ever before, a social rather than a strictly individual activity. It takes place in a context of government and corporate organisation and funding. It relies on public and corporate medical research and product development for

> "Medicine is today, more than ever before, a social rather than a strictly individual activity."

its knowledge base and treatments. It requires complex healthcare institutions for many of its procedures. It treats diseases and illnesses that are as much social as biological in origin.

The Hippocratic tradition of medical ethics has little guidance to offer with regard to relationships with society. To supplement this tradition, present-day medical ethics addresses the issues that arise beyond the individual patient-physician relationship and provides criteria and processes for dealing with these issues.

To speak of the 'social' character of medicine immediately raises the question – what is society? In this Manual the term refers to a community or nation. It is not synonymous with government; governments should, but often do not, represent the interests of society, but even when they do, they are acting **for** society, not **as** society.

Physicians have various relationships with society. Because society, and its physical environment, are important factors in the health of patients, both the medical profession in general and individual physicians have significant roles to play in public health, health education, environmental protection, laws affecting the health or well-being of the community, and testimony at judicial proceedings. As the WMA **Declaration on the Rights of the Patient** puts it: "Whenever legislation, government action or any other administration or institution denies patients [their] rights, physicians should pursue appropriate means to assure or to restore them." Physicians are also called upon to play a major role in the allocation of society's scarce healthcare resources, and sometimes they have a duty to prevent patients from accessing services to which they are not entitled. Implementing these responsibilities can raise ethical conflicts, especially when the interests of society seem to conflict with those of individual patients.

## DUAL LOYALTY

When physicians have responsibilities and are accountable both to their patients and to a third party and when these responsibilities and accountabilities are incompatible, they find themselves in a situation of 'dual loyalty'. Third parties that demand physician loyalty include governments, employers (e.g., hospitals and managed healthcare organizations), insurers, military officials, police, prison officials and family members. Although the WMA **International Code of Medical Ethics** states that "A physician shall owe his patients complete loyalty," it is generally accepted that physicians may in exceptional situations have to place the interests of others above those of the patient. The ethical challenge is to decide when and how to protect the patient in the face of pressures from third parties.

> "...physicians may in exceptional situations have to place the interests of others above those of the patient."

Dual loyalty situations comprise a spectrum ranging from those where society's interests should take precedence to those where the patient's interests are clearly paramount. In between is a large grey area where the right course of action requires considerable discernment.

At one end of the spectrum are requirements for mandatory reporting of patients who suffer from designated diseases, those deemed not fit to drive or those suspected of child abuse. Physicians should fulfil these requirements without hesitation, although patients should be informed that such reporting will take place.

At the other end of the spectrum are requests or orders by the police or military to take part in practices that violate fundamental human rights, such as torture. In its 2003 **Resolution on the Responsibility of Physicians in the Denunciation of Acts of Torture or Cruel or Inhuman or Degrading Treatment of which They are Aware**, the WMA provides specific guidance to physicians who are in this situation. In particular, physicians should guard their professional independence to determine the best interests of the patient and should observe, as far as possible, the normal ethical requirements of informed consent and confidentiality. Any breach of these requirements must be justified and must be disclosed to the patient. Physicians should report to the appropriate authorities any unjustified interference in the care of their patients, especially if fundamental human rights are being denied. If the authorities are unresponsive, help may be available from a national medical association, the WMA and human rights organizations.

> "Physicians should report to the appropriate authorities any unjustified interference in the care of their patients, especially if fundamental human rights are being denied."

Closer to the middle of the spectrum are the practices of some managed healthcare programmes that limit the clinical autonomy of physicians to determine how their patients should be treated. Although such practices are not necessarily contrary to the best interests of patients, they can be, and physicians need to consider carefully whether they should participate in such programmes. If they have no choice in the matter, for example, where there are no alternative programmes, they should *advocate* vigorously for their own patients and, through their medical associations, for the needs of all the patients affected by such restrictive policies.

A particular form of a dual loyalty issue faced by physicians is the potential or actual conflict of interest between a commercial organization on the one hand and patients and/or society on the other. Pharmaceutical companies, medical device manufacturers and other commercial organizations frequently offer physicians gifts and other benefits that range from free samples to travel and accommodation at educational events to excessive remuneration for research activities (see Chapter Five). A common underlying motive for such company largesse is to convince the physician to prescribe or use the company's products, which may not be the best ones for the physician's patients and/or may add unnecessarily to a society's health costs. The WMA's 2004 **Statement Concerning the Relationship between Physicians and Commercial Enterprises** provides guidelines for physicians in such situations and many national medical associations have their own guidelines. The primary ethical principle underlying these guidelines is that physicians should resolve any conflict between their own interests and those of their patients in their patients' favour.

> "...physicians should resolve any conflict between their own interests and those of their patients in their patients' favour."

## RESOURCE ALLOCATION

In every country in the world, including the richest ones, there is an already wide and steadily increasing gap between the needs and desires for healthcare services and the availability of resources to provide these services. The existence of this gap requires that the existing resources be rationed in some manner. Healthcare rationing, or 'resource allocation' as it is more commonly referred to, takes place at three levels:

- At the highest ('macro') level, governments decide how much of the overall budget should be allocated to health; which healthcare expenses will be provided at no charge and which will require payment either directly from patients or from their medical insurance plans; within the health budget, how much will go to remuneration for physicians, nurses and other heath care workers, to capital and operating expenses for hospitals and other institutions, to research, to education of health professionals, to treatment of specific conditions such as tuberculosis or AIDS, and so on.

- At the institutional ('meso') level, which includes hospitals, clinics, healthcare agencies, etc., authorities decide how to allocate their resources: which services to provide; how much to spend on staff, equipment, security, other operating expenses, renovations, expansion, etc.

- At the individual patient ('micro') level, healthcare providers, especially physicians, decide what tests should be ordered, whether a referral to another physician is needed, whether the patient should be hospitalised, whether a brand-name drug is required rather than a generic one, etc. It has been estimated that physicians are responsible for initiating 80% of healthcare expenditures, and despite the growing encroachment of managed care, they still have considerable discretion as to which resources their patients will have access.

The choices that are made at each level have a major ethical component, since they are based on values and have significant consequences for the health and well-being of individuals and communities. Although individual physicians are affected by decisions at all levels, they have the greatest involvement at the micro-level. Accordingly, this will be the focus of what follows.

As noted above, physicians were traditionally expected to act solely in the interests of their own patients, without regard to the needs of others. Their primary ethical values of compassion, competence and autonomy were directed towards serving the needs of their own patients. This individualistic approach to medical ethics survived the transition from physician paternalism to patient autonomy, where the will of the individual patient became the main criterion for deciding what resources he or she should receive. More recently, however, another value, justice, has become an important factor in medical decision-making. It entails a more social approach to the distribution of resources, one that considers the needs of other patients. According to this approach, physicians are responsible not just for their own patients but, to a certain extent, for others as well.

> "...physicians are responsible not just for their own patients but, to a certain extent, for others as well. "

This new understanding of the physician's role in allocating resources is expressed in many national medical association codes of ethics and, as well, in the WMA **Declaration on the Rights of the Patient**, which states: "In circumstances where a choice must be made between potential patients for a particular treatment which is in limited supply, all such patients are entitled to a fair selection procedure for that treatment. That choice must be based on medical criteria and made without discrimination."

One way that physicians can exercise their responsibility for the allocation of resources is by avoiding wasteful and inefficient practices, even when patients request them. The overuse of antibiotics is just one example of a practice that is both wasteful and harmful. Many other common treatments have been shown in randomized clinical trials to be ineffective for the conditions for which they are used. Clinical practice guidelines are available for many medical conditions; they help to distinguish between effective and ineffective treatments. Physicians should familiarize themselves with these guidelines, both to conserve resources and to provide optimal treatment to their patients.

> "One way that physicians can exercise their responsibility for the allocation of resources is by avoiding wasteful and inefficient practices, even when patients request them. "

A type of allocation decision that many physicians must make is the choice between two or more patients who are in need of a scarce resource such as emergency staff attention, the one remaining intensive care bed, organs for transplantation, high-tech radiological tests, and certain very expensive drugs. Physicians who exercise control over these resources must decide which patients will have access to them and which will not, knowing full well that those who are denied may suffer, and even die, as a result.

Some physicians face an additional conflict in allocating resources, in that they play a role in formulating general policies that affect their own patients, among others. This conflict occurs in hospitals and other institutions where physicians hold administrative positions or serve on committees where policies are recommended or determined. Although many physicians attempt to detach themselves from their preoccupation with their own patients, others may try to use their position to advance the cause of their patients over others with greater needs.

aling with these allocation issues, physicians must not only balance the principles of compassion and justice but, in doing so, must decide which approach to justice is preferable. There are several such approaches, including the following:

- **LIBERTARIAN** – resources should be distributed according to market principles (individual choice conditioned by ability and willingness to pay, with limited charity care for the destitute);

- **UTILITARIAN** – resources should be distributed according to the principle of maximum benefit for all;

- **EGALITARIAN** – resources should be distributed strictly according to need;

- **RESTORATIVE** – resources should be distributed so as to favour the historically disadvantaged.

As noted above, physicians have been gradually moving away from the traditional individualism of medical ethics, which would favour the libertarian approach, towards a more social conception of their role. Even if the libertarian approach is generally rejected, however, medical ethicists have reached no consensus on which of the other three approaches is superior. Each one clearly has very different results when applied to the issues mentioned above, that is, deciding what tests should be ordered, whether a referral to another physician is needed, whether the patient should be hospitalised, whether a brand-name drug is required rather than a generic one, who gets the organ for transplantation, etc. The utilitarian approach is probably the most difficult for individual physicians to practise, since it requires a great deal of data on the probable outcomes of different interventions, not just for the physician's own patients but for all others. The choice between the other two (or three, if the libertarian is included) will depend on the physician's own personal morality as well as the socio-political environment in which he or

> "...choice ...will depend on the physician's own personal morality as well as the socio-political environment in which he or she practises."

she practises. Some countries, such as the U.S.A., favour the libertarian approach; others, e.g., Sweden, are known for their egalitarianism; while still others, such as South Africa, are attempting a restorative approach. Many health planners promote utilitarianism. Despite their differences, two or more of these concepts of justice often coexist in national health systems, and in these countries physicians may be able to choose a practice setting (e.g., public or private) that accords with their own approach.

In addition to whatever roles physicians may have in allocating existing healthcare resources, they also have a responsibility to advocate for expansion of these resources where they are insufficient to meet patient needs. This usually requires that physicians work together, in their professional associations, to convince decision-makers in government and elsewhere of the existence of these needs and how best to meet them, both within their own countries and globally.

> "...physicians ...have a responsibility to advocate for expansion of these resources where they are insufficient to meet patient needs."

## PUBLIC HEALTH

20th century medicine witnessed the emergence of an unfortunate division between 'public health' and other healthcare (presumably 'private' or 'individual' health). It is unfortunate because, as noted above, the public is made up of individuals, and measures designed to protect and enhance the health of the public result in health benefits for individuals.

Confusion also arises if 'public health' is taken to mean 'publicly-funded healthcare' (i.e., healthcare funded through a country's taxation system or a compulsory universal insurance system) and seen as the opposite of 'privately-funded healthcare' (i.e., healthcare paid for by the individual or through private health insurance and usually not universally available).

The term 'public health', as understood here, refers both to the health of the public and also to the medical specialty that deals with health from a population perspective rather than on an individual basis. There is a great need for specialists in this field in every country to advise on and advocate for public policies that promote good health as well as to engage in activities to protect the public from communicable diseases and other health hazards. The practice of public health (sometimes called 'public health medicine' or 'community medicine') relies heavily for its scientific basis on **epidemiology**, which is the study of the distribution and determinants of health and disease in populations. Indeed, some physicians go on to take extra academic training and become medical epidemiologists. However, all physicians need to be aware of the social and environmental determinants that influence the health status of their individual patients. As the WMA **Statement on Health Promotion** notes: "Medical practitioners and their professional associations have an ethical duty and professional responsibility to act in the best interests of their patients at all times and to integrate this responsibility with a broader concern for and involvement in promoting and assuring the health of the public."

> "all physicians need to be aware of the social and environmental determinants that influence the health status of their individual patients."

Public health measures such as vaccination campaigns and emergency responses to outbreaks of contagious diseases are important factors in the health of individuals but social factors such as housing, nutrition and employment are equally, if not more, significant. Physicians are seldom able to treat the social causes of their individual patients' illnesses, although they should refer the patients to whatever social services are available. However, they can contribute, even if indirectly, to long-term solutions to these problems by participating in public health and health education activities, monitoring and reporting environmental hazards, identifying and publicizing adverse health effects from social problems such as abuse and violence, and advocating for improvements in public health services.

Sometimes, though, the interests of public health may conflict with those of individual patients, for example, when a vaccination that carries a risk of an adverse reaction will prevent an individual from transmitting a disease but not from contracting it, or when notification is required for certain contagious diseases, for cases of child or elder abuse, or for conditions that may render certain activities, such as driving a car or piloting an aircraft, dangerous to the individual and to others. These are examples of dual-loyalty situations as described above. Procedures for dealing with these and related situations are discussed under 'confidentiality' in Chapter Two of this Manual. In general, physicians should attempt to find ways to minimise any harm that individual patients might suffer as a result of meeting public health requirements. For example, when reporting is required, the patient's confidentiality should be protected to the greatest extent possible while fulfilling the legal requirements.

A different type of conflict between the interests of individual patients and those of society arises when physicians are asked to assist patients to receive benefits to which they are not entitled, for example, insurance payments or sick-leave. Physicians have been vested with the authority to certify that patients have the appropriate medical condition that would qualify them for such benefits. Although some physicians are unwilling to deny requests from patients for certificates that do not apply in their circumstances, they should rather help their patients find other means of support that do not require unethical behaviour.

## GLOBAL HEALTH

The recognition that physicians have responsibilities to the society in which they live has been expanded in recent years to include a responsibility for global health. This term has been defined as health problems, issues and concerns that transcend national boundaries, that may be influenced by circumstances or experiences in other countries, and that are best addressed by cooperative actions and solutions. Global health is part of the much larger movement of globalization that encompasses information exchange, commerce, politics, tourism and many other human activities.

The basis of globalization is the recognition that individuals and societies are increasingly interdependent. This is clearly evident with regard to human health, as the rapid spread of diseases such as influenza and SARS has shown. Such epidemics require international action for their control. The failure to recognize and treat highly contagious diseases by a physician in one country can have devastating effects on patients in other countries. For this reason, the ethical obligations of physicians extend far beyond their individual patients and even their communities and nations.

> "The failure to recognize and treat highly contagious diseases by a physician in one country can have devastating effects on patients in other countries."

The development of a global view of health has resulted in an increasing awareness of health disparities throughout the world. Despite large-scale campaigns to combat premature mortality and debilitating morbidity in the poorest countries, which have resulted in certain success stories such as the elimination of smallpox and (hopefully) polio, the gap in health status between high and low-income countries continues to widen. This is partly due to HIV/AIDS, which has had its worst effects in poor countries, but it is also due to the failure of low-income countries to benefit from the increase in wealth that the world as a whole has experienced during the past decades. Although the causes of poverty are largely political and economic and are therefore far beyond the control of physicians and their associations, physicians do have to deal with the ill-health that is the result of poverty. In low-income countries physicians have few resources to offer these patients and are constantly faced with the challenge of allocating these resources in the fairest way. Even in middle- and high-income countries, though, physicians encounter patients who are directly affected by globalization, such as refugees, and who sometimes do not have access to the medical coverage that citizens of those countries enjoy.

Another feature of globalization is the international mobility of health professionals, including physicians. The outflow of physicians from developing to highly industrialized countries has been advantageous for both the physicians and the receiving countries but not so for the exporting countries. The WMA, in its **Ethical Guidelines for the International Recruitment of Physicians**, states that physicians should not be prevented from leaving their home or adopted country to pursue career opportunities in another country. It does, however, call on every country to do its utmost to educate an adequate number of physicians, taking into account its needs and resources, and not to rely on immigration from other countries to meet its need for physicians.

Physicians in the industrialized countries have a long tradition of providing their experience and skills to developing countries.

This takes many forms: emergency medical aid coordinated by organizations such as the Red Cross and Red Crescent Societies and Médecins sans Frontières, short-term surgical campaigns to deal with conditions such as cataracts or cleft palates, visiting faculty appointments in medical schools, short- or long-term medical research projects, provision of medicines and medical equipment, etc. Such programmes exemplify the positive side of globalization and serve to redress, at least partially, the movement of physicians from poorer to wealthier countries.

# BACK TO THE CASE STUDY

According to the analysis of the physician-society relationship presented in this chapter, Dr. S is right to consider the impact on society of her patient's behaviour. Even if the consultations with the other health practitioner occur outside of the health system in which Dr. S works and therefore do not entail any financial cost to society, the patient is taking up Dr. S's time that could be devoted to other patients in need of her services. However, physicians such as Dr. S must be cautious in dealing with situations such as this. Patients are often unable to make fully rational decisions for a variety of reasons and may need considerable time and health education to come to an understanding of what is in the best interests of themselves and of others. Dr. S is also right to approach her medical association to seek a societal solution to this problem, since it affects not just herself and this one patient but other physicians and patients as well.

# CHAPTER FOUR –
# PHYSICIANS AND COLLEAGUES

Medical team going over a case
© Pete Saloutos/CORBIS

## OBJECTIVES

After working through this chapter you should be able to:

- describe how physicians should behave towards one another
- justify reporting unethical behaviour of colleagues
- identify the main ethical principles relating to cooperation with others in the care of patients
- explain how to resolve conflicts with other healthcare providers

## CASE STUDY #3

Dr. C, a newly appointed anaesthetist in a city hospital, is alarmed by the behaviour of the senior surgeon in the operating room. The surgeon uses out-of-date techniques that prolong operations and result in greater post-operative pain and longer recovery times. Moreover, he makes frequent crude jokes about the patients that obviously bother the assisting nurses. As a more junior staff member, Dr. C is reluctant to criticize the surgeon personally or to report him to higher authorities. However, he feels that he must do something to improve the situation.

### CHALLENGES TO MEDICAL AUTHORITY

Physicians belong to a profession that has traditionally functioned in an extremely *hierarchical* fashion, both internally and externally. Internally, there are three overlapping *hierarchies*: the first differentiates among specialties, with some being considered more prestigious, and

> "Physicians belong to a profession that has traditionally functioned in an extremely *hierarchical* fashion"

better remunerated, than others; the second is within specialties, with academics being more influential than those in private or public practice; the third relates to the care of specific patients, where the primary caregiver is at the top of the hierarchy and other physicians, even those with greater seniority and/or skills, serve simply as consultants unless the patient is transferred to their care. Externally, physicians have traditionally been at the top of the hierarchy of caregivers, above nurses and other health professionals.

This chapter will deal with ethical issues that arise in both internal and external hierarchies. Some issues are common to both; others are found only in one or the other. Many of these issues are relatively new, since they result from recent changes in medicine and health-care. A brief description of these changes is in order, since they pose major challenges to the traditional exercise of medical authority.

With the rapid growth in scientific knowledge and its clinical applications, medicine has become increasingly complex. Individual physicians cannot possibly be experts in all their patients' diseases and potential treatments and they need the assistance of other specialist physicians and skilled health professionals such as nurses, pharmacists, physiotherapists, laboratory technicians, social workers and many others. Physicians need to know how to access the relevant skills that their patients require and that they themselves lack.

As discussed in Chapter Two, medical paternalism has been gradually eroded by the increasing recognition of the right of patients to make their own medical decisions. As a result, a cooperative model of decision-making has replaced the authoritarian model that was characteristic of traditional medical paternalism. The same thing is happening in relationships between physicians and other health professionals. The latter are increasingly unwilling to follow physicians' orders without knowing the reasons behind the orders. They see themselves as professionals with

"...a cooperative model of decision-making has replaced the authoritarian model that was characteristic of traditional medical paternalism."

specific ethical responsibilities towards patients; if their perception of these responsibilities conflicts with the physician's orders, they feel that they must question or even challenge the orders. Whereas under the hierarchical model of authority, there was never any doubt about who was in charge and who should prevail when conflict occurred, the cooperative model can give rise to disputes about appropriate patient care.

Developments such as these are changing the 'rules of the game' for the relationships of physicians with their medical colleagues and other health professionals. The remainder of this chapter will identify some problematic aspects of these relationships and suggest ways of dealing with them.

## RELATIONSHIPS WITH PHYSICIAN COLLEAGUES, TEACHERS AND STUDENTS

As members of the medical profession, physicians have traditionally been expected to treat each other more as family members than as strangers or even as friends. The WMA **Declaration of Geneva** includes the pledge, "My colleagues will be my sisters and brothers." The interpretation of this requirement has varied from country to country and over time. For example, where fee-for-service was the principal or only form of remuneration for physicians, there was a strong tradition of 'professional courtesy' whereby physicians did not charge their colleagues for medical treatment. This practice has declined in countries where third-party reimbursement is available.

Besides the positive requirements to treat one's colleagues respectfully and to work cooperatively to maximize patient care, the WMA **International Code of Medical Ethics** contains two restrictions on physicians' relationships with one another: (1) paying or receiving any fee or any other consideration solely to procure the referral of a patient; and (2) stealing patients from colleagues. A third obligation, to report unethical or incompetent behaviour by colleagues, is discussed below.

In the Hippocratic tradition of medical ethics, physicians owe special respect to their teachers. The **Declaration of Geneva** puts it this way: "I will give to my teachers the respect and gratitude which is their due." Although present-day medical education involves multiple student-teacher interactions rather than the one-on-one relationship of former times, it is still dependent on the good will and dedication of practising physicians, who often receive no remuneration for their teaching activities. Medical students and other medical trainees owe a debt of gratitude to their teachers, without whom medical education would be reduced to self-instruction.

For their part, teachers have an obligation to treat their students respectfully and to serve as good role models in dealing with patients. The so-called 'hidden curriculum' of medical education, i.e., the standards of behaviour exhibited by practising physicians, is much more influential than the explicit curriculum of medical

> **"...teachers have an obligation to treat their students respectfully and to serve as good role models in dealing with patients."**

ethics, and if there is a conflict between the requirements of ethics and the attitudes and behaviour of their teachers, medical students are more likely to follow their teachers' example.

Teachers have a particular obligation not to require students to engage in unethical practices. Examples of such practices that have been reported in medical journals include medical students obtaining patient consent for medical treatment in situations where a fully qualified health professional should do this, performing pelvic examinations on anaesthetized or newly dead patients without consent, and performing unsupervised procedures that, although minor (e.g., I-V insertion), are considered by some students to be beyond their competence. Given the unequal power balance between students and teachers and the consequent reluctance of

> "Students concerned about ethical aspects of their education should have access to such mechanisms where they can raise concerns"

students to question or refuse such orders, teachers need to ensure that they are not requiring students to act unethically. In many medical schools, there are class representatives or medical student associations that, among their other roles, may be able to raise concerns about ethical issues in medical education. Students concerned about ethical aspects of their education should have access to such mechanisms where they can raise concerns without necessarily being identified as the *whistle-blower,* as well as access to appropriate support if it becomes necessary to take the issue to a more formal process.

For their part, medical students are expected to exhibit high standards of ethical behaviour as appropriate for future physicians. They should treat other students as colleagues and be prepared to offer help when it is needed, including corrective advice in regard to unprofessional behaviour. They should also contribute fully to shared projects and duties such as study assignments and on-call service.

## REPORTING UNSAFE OR UNETHICAL PRACTICES

Medicine has traditionally taken pride in its status as a self-regulating profession. In return for the privileges accorded to it by society and the trust given to its members by their patients, the medical profession has established high standards of behaviour for its members and disciplinary procedures to investigate accusations of misbehaviour and, if necessary, to punish the wrongdoers. This system of self-regulation has often failed, and in recent years steps have been taken to make the profession more accountable, for example, by appointing lay members to regulatory authorities. The main requirement for self-regulation, however, is wholehearted support by physicians for its principles and their willingness to recognise and deal with unsafe and unethical practices.

This obligation to report incompetence, impairment or misconduct of one's colleagues is emphasised in codes of medical ethics. For example, the WMA **International Code of Medical Ethics** states that "A physician shall... strive to expose those physicians deficient in character or competence, or who engage in fraud or deception." The application of this principle is seldom easy, however. On the one hand, a physician may be tempted to attack the reputation of a colleague for unworthy personal motives, such as jealousy, or in retaliation for a perceived insult by the colleague. A physician may also be reluctant to report a colleague's misbehaviour because of friendship or sympathy ("there but for the grace of God go I"). The consequences of such reporting can be very detrimental to the one who reports, including almost certain hostility on the part of the accused and possibly other colleagues as well.

Despite these drawbacks to reporting wrongdoing, it is a professional duty of physicians. Not only are they responsible for maintaining the good reputation of the profession, but they are often the only ones who recognise incompetence, impairment or misconduct. However, reporting colleagues to the disciplinary authority should normally be a last resort after other alternatives have been tried and found wanting. The first step might be to approach the colleague and say that you consider his or her behaviour

> "...reporting colleagues to the disciplinary authority should normally be a last resort after other alternatives have been tried and found wanting"

unsafe or unethical. If the matter can be resolved at that level, there may be no need to go farther. If not, the next step might be to discuss the matter with your and/or the offender's supervisor and leave the decision about further action to that person. If this tactic is not practical or does not succeed, then it may be necessary to take the final step of informing the disciplinary authority.

## RELATIONSHIPS WITH OTHER HEALTH PROFESSIONALS

Chapter Two on relationships with patients began with a discussion of the great importance of respect and equal treatment in the physician-patient relationship. The principles set forth in that discussion are equally relevant for relationships with co-workers. In particular, the prohibition against discrimination on grounds such as "age, disease or disability, creed, ethnic origin, gender, nationality, political affiliation, race, sexual orientation, or social standing" (WMA **Declaration of Geneva**) is applicable in dealings with all those with whom physicians interact in caring for patients and other professional activities.

Non-discrimination is a passive characteristic of a relationship. Respect is something more active and positive. With regard to other healthcare providers, whether physicians, nurses, auxiliary health workers, etc., it entails an appreciation of their skills and experience insofar as these can contribute to the care of patients. All healthcare providers are not equal in terms of their education and training, but they do share a basic human equality as well as similar concern for the well-being of patients.

As with patients, though, there are legitimate grounds for refusing to enter or for terminating a relationship with another healthcare provider. These include lack of confidence in the ability or integrity of the other person and serious personality clashes. Distinguishing these from less worthy motives can require considerable ethical sensitivity on the physician's part.

# COOPERATION

Medicine is at the same time a highly individualistic and a highly cooperative profession. On the one hand, physicians are quite possessive of 'their' patients. It is claimed, with good reason, that the individual physician-patient relationship is the best means of attaining the knowledge of the patient and continuity of care that are optimal for the prevention and treatment of illness. The retention of patients also benefits the physician, at least financially. At the same time, as described above, medicine is highly complex and specialized, thus requiring close cooperation among practitioners with different but complementary knowledge and skills. This tension between individualism and cooperation has been a recurrent theme in medical ethics.

The weakening of medical paternalism has been accompanied by the disappearance of the belief that physicians 'own' their patients. The traditional right of patients to ask for a second opinion has been expanded to include access to other healthcare providers who may be better able to meet their needs. According to the WMA **Declaration on the Rights of the Patient**, "The physician has an obligation to cooperate in the coordination of medically indicated care with other healthcare providers treating the patient." However, as noted above, physicians are not to profit from this cooperation by fee-splitting.

> "The weakening of medical paternalism has been accompanied by the disappearance of the belief that physicians 'own' their patients."

These restrictions on the physician's 'ownership' of patients need to be counterbalanced by other measures that are intended to safeguard the primacy of the patient-physician relationship. For example, a patient who is being treated by more than one physician, which is usually the case in a hospital, should, wherever possible, have one physician coordinating the care who can keep the patient informed about his or her overall progress and help the patient make decisions.

Whereas relationships among physicians are governed by generally well-formulated and understood rules, relationships between physicians and other healthcare professionals are in a state of flux and there is considerable disagreement about what their respective roles should be. As noted above, many nurses, pharmacists, physiotherapists and other professionals consider themselves to be more competent in their areas of patient care than are physicians and see no reason why they should not be treated as equals to physicians. They favour a team approach to patient care in which the views of all caregivers are given equal consideration, and they consider themselves accountable to the patient, not to the physician. Many physicians, on the other hand, feel that even if the team approach is adopted, there has to be one person in charge, and physicians are best suited for that role given their education and experience.

Although some physicians may resist challenges to their traditional, almost absolute, authority, it seems certain that their role will change in response to claims by both patients and other healthcare providers for greater participation in medical decision-making. Physicians will have to be able to justify their recommendations to others and persuade them to accept these recommendations. In addition to these communication skills, physicians will need to be able to resolve conflicts that arise among the different participants in the care of the patient.

A particular challenge to cooperation in the best interests of patients results from their recourse to traditional or alternative health providers ('healers'). These individuals are consulted by a large proportion of the population in Africa and Asia and increasingly so in Europe and the Americas. Although some would consider the two approaches as complementary, in many situations they may be in conflict. Since at least some of the traditional and alternative interventions have therapeutic effects and are sought out by patients, physicians should explore ways of cooperation with their practitioners. How this can be done will vary from one country to another and from one type of practitioner to another. In all such interactions the well-being of patients should be the primary consideration.

## CONFLICT RESOLUTION

Although physicians can experience many different types of conflicts with other physicians and healthcare providers, for example, over office procedures or remuneration, the focus here will be on conflicts about patient care. Ideally, healthcare decisions will reflect agreement among the patient, physicians and all others involved in the patient's care. However, uncertainty and diverse viewpoints can give rise to disagreement about the goals of care or the means of achieving those goals. Limited healthcare resources and organisational policies may also make it difficult to achieve consensus.

> "...uncertainty and diverse viewpoints can give rise to disagreement about the goals of care or the means of achieving those goals."

Disagreements among healthcare providers about the goals of care and treatment or the means of achieving those goals should be clarified and resolved by the members of the healthcare team so as not to compromise their relationships with the patient. Disagreements between healthcare providers and administrators with regard to the allocation of resources should be resolved within the facility or agency and not be debated in the presence of the patient. Since both types of conflicts are ethical in nature, their resolution can benefit from the advice of a clinical ethics committee or an ethics consultant where such resources are available.

The following guidelines can be useful for resolving such conflicts:

- Conflicts should be resolved as informally as possible, for example, through direct negotiation between the persons who disagree, moving to more formal procedures only when informal measures have been unsuccessful.

- The opinions of all those directly involved should be elicited and given respectful consideration.

- The informed choice of the patient, or authorized substitute decision-maker, regarding treatment should be the primary consideration in resolving disputes.

- If the dispute is about which options the patient should be offered, a broader rather than a narrower range of options is usually preferable. If a preferred treatment is not available because of resource limitations, the patient should normally be informed of this.

- If, after reasonable effort, agreement or compromise cannot be reached through dialogue, the decision of the person with the right or responsibility for making the decision should be accepted. If it is unclear or disputed who has the right or responsibility to make the decision, mediation, arbitration or adjudication should be sought.

If healthcare providers cannot support the decision that prevails as a matter of professional judgement or personal morality, they should be allowed to withdraw from participation in carrying out the decision, after ensuring that the person receiving care is not at risk of harm or abandonment.

## BACK TO THE CASE STUDY

Dr. C is right to be alarmed by the behaviour of the senior surgeon in the operating room. Not only is he endangering the health of the patient but he is being disrespectful to both the patient and his colleagues. Dr. C has an ethical duty not to ignore this behaviour but to do something about it. As a first step, he should not indicate any support for the offensive behaviour, for example, by laughing at the jokes. If he thinks that discussing the matter with the surgeon might be effective, he should go ahead and do this. Otherwise, he may have to go directly to higher authorities in the hospital. If they are unwilling to deal with the situation, then he can approach the appropriate physician licensing body and ask it to investigate.

# CHAPTER FIVE –
# ETHICS AND MEDICAL RESEARCH

Sleeping sickness is back
© Robert Patric/CORBIS SYGMA

## OBJECTIVES

After working through this chapter you should be able to:

· identify the main principles of research ethics
· know how to balance research and clinical care
· satisfy the requirements of ethics review committees

## CASE STUDY #4

Dr. R, a general practitioner in a small rural town, is approached by a contract research organization (C.R.O.) to participate in a clinical trial of a new non-steroidal anti-inflammatory drug (NSAID) for osteoarthritis. She is offered a sum of money for each patient that she enrols in the trial. The C.R.O. representative assures her that the trial has received all the necessary approvals, including one from an ethics review committee. Dr. R has never participated in a trial before and is pleased to have this opportunity, especially with the extra money. She accepts without inquiring further about the scientific or ethical aspects of the trial.

### IMPORTANCE OF MEDICAL RESEARCH

Medicine is not an exact science in the way that mathematics and physics are. It does have many general principles that are valid most of the time, but every patient is different and what is an effective

> "...medicine is inherently experimental"

treatment for 90% of the population may not work for the other 10%. Thus, medicine is inherently experimental. Even the most widely accepted treatments need to be monitored and evaluated to determine whether they are effective for specific patients and, for that matter, for patients in general. This is one of the functions of medical research.

Another, perhaps better known, function is the development of new treatments, especially drugs, medical devices and surgical techniques. Great progress has been made in this area over the past 50 years and today there is more medical research underway than ever before. Nevertheless, there are still many unanswered questions about the functioning of the human body, the causes of diseases (both familiar and novel ones) and the best ways to prevent or cure them. Medical research is the only means of answering these questions.

In addition to seeking a better understanding of human physiology, medical research investigates a wide variety of other factors in human health, including patterns of disease (epidemiology), the organization, funding and delivery of healthcare (health systems research), social and cultural aspects of health (medical sociology and anthropology), law (legal medicine) and ethics (medical ethics). The importance of these types of research is being increasingly recognized by funding agencies, many of which have specific programs for non-physiological medical research.

## RESEARCH IN MEDICAL PRACTICE

All physicians make use of the results of medical research in their clinical practice. To maintain their competence, physicians must keep up with the current research in their area of practice through Continuing Medical Education/ Continuing Professional Development programs, medical journals and interaction with knowledgeable colleagues. Even if they do not engage in research themselves, physicians must know how to interpret the results of research and apply them to their patients. Thus, a basic familiarity with research methods is essential for competent medical practice. The best way to gain this familiarity

> "Even if they do not engage in research themselves, physicians must know how to interpret the results of research and apply them to their patients."

is to take part in a research project, either as a medical student or following qualification.

The most common method of research for practising physicians is the clinical trial. Before a new drug can be approved by government-mandated regulatory authorities, it must undergo extensive testing for safety and efficacy. The process begins with laboratory studies followed by testing on animals. If this proves promising, the four steps, or phases, of clinical research, are next:

- Phase one research, usually conducted on a relatively small number of healthy volunteers, who are often paid for their participation, is intended to determine what dosage of the drug is required to produce a response in the human body, how the body processes the drug, and whether the drug produces toxic or harmful effects.

- Phase two research is conducted on a group of patients who have the disease that the drug is intended to treat. Its goals are to determine whether the drug has any beneficial effect on the disease and has any harmful side effects.

- Phase three research is the clinical trial, in which the drug is administered to a large number of patients and compared to another drug, if there is one for the condition in question, and/or to a placebo. Where possible, such trials are 'double-blinded', i.e., neither research subjects nor their physicians know who is receiving which drug or placebo.

- Phase four research takes place after the drug is licensed and marketed. For the first few years, a new drug is monitored for side effects that did not show up in the earlier phases. Additionally, the pharmaceutical company is usually interested in how well the drug is being received by physicians who prescribe it and patients who take it.

The rapid increase in recent years in the number of ongoing trials has required finding and enrolling ever-larger numbers of patients to meet the statistical requirements of the trials. Those in charge of the trials, whether independent physicians or pharmaceutical companies, now rely on many other physicians, often in different countries, to enrol patients as research subjects.

Although such participation in research is valuable experience for physicians, there are potential problems that must be recognized and avoided. In the first place, the physician's role in the physician-patient relationship is different from the researcher's role in the researcher-research subject relationship, even if the physician and the researcher are the same person. The physician's primary responsibility is the health and well-being of the patient, whereas the researcher's primary responsibility is the generation of knowledge, which may or may not contribute to the research subject's health and well-being. Thus, there is a potential for conflict between the two roles. When this occurs, the physician role must take precedence over the researcher. What this means in practice will be evident below.

> "...the physician's role in the physician-patient relationship is different from the researcher's role in the researcher-research subject relationship"

Another potential problem in combining these two roles is conflict of interest. Medical research is a well-funded enterprise, and physicians are sometimes offered considerable rewards for participating. These can include cash payments for enrolling research subjects, equipment such as computers to transmit the research data, invitations to conferences to discuss the research findings, and co-authorship of publications on the results of the research. The physician's interest in obtaining these benefits can sometimes conflict with the duty to provide the patient with the best available treatment. It can also conflict with the right of the patient to receive all the necessary information to make a fully informed decision whether or not to participate in a research study.

These potential problems can be overcome. The ethical values of the physician – compassion, competence, autonomy – apply to the medical researcher as well. So there is no inherent conflict between the two roles. As long as physicians understand and follow the basic rules of research ethics, they should have no difficulty participating in research as an integral component of their clinical practice.

## ETHICAL REQUIREMENTS

The basic principles of research ethics are well established. It was not always so, however. Many prominent medical researchers in the 19th and 20th centuries conducted experiments on patients without their consent and with little if any concern for the patients' well-being. Although there were some statements of research ethics dating from the early 20th century, they did not prevent physicians in Nazi Germany and elsewhere from performing research on subjects that clearly violated fundamental human rights. Following World War Two, some of these physicians were tried and convicted by a special tribunal at Nuremberg, Germany. The basis of the judgment is known as the Nuremberg Code, which has served as one of the foundational documents of modern research ethics. Among the ten principles of this Code is the requirement of voluntary consent if a patient is to serve as a research subject.

The World Medical Association was established in 1947, the same year that the Nuremberg Code was set forth. Conscious of the violations of medical ethics before and during World War Two, the founders of the WMA immediately took steps to ensure that physicians would at least be aware of their ethical obligations. In 1954, after several years of study, the WMA adopted a set of **Principles for Those in Research and Experimentation**. This document was revised over the next ten years and eventually was adopted as the **Declaration of Helsinki (DoH)** in 1964. It was further revised in 1975, 1983, 1989, 1996 and 2000. The DoH is a concise summary of research ethics. Other, much more detailed, documents have been produced in recent years on research ethics in general (e.g., Council for International Organizations of Medical Sciences, **International Ethical Guidelines for Biomedical Research Involving Human Subjects**, 1993, revised in 2002) and on specific topics in research ethics (e.g., Nuffield Council on Bioethics [UK], **The Ethics of Research Related to Healthcare in Developing Countries**, 2002).

Despite the different scope, length and authorship of these documents, they agree to a very large extent on the basic principles of research ethics. These principles have been incorporated in the laws and/or regulations of many countries and international organizations, including those that deal with the approval of drugs and medical devices. Here is a brief description of the principles, taken primarily from the **DoH**:

## Ethics Review Committee Approval

Paragraphs 13 and 14 of the **DoH** stipulate that every proposal for medical research on human subjects must be reviewed and approved by an independent ethics committee before it can proceed. In order to obtain approval, researchers must

> "...every proposal for medical research on human subjects must be reviewed and approved by an independent ethics committee before it can proceed."

explain the purpose and methodology of the project; demonstrate how research subjects will be recruited, how their consent will be obtained and how their privacy will be protected; specify how the project is being funded; and disclose any potential conflicts of interest on the part of the researchers. The ethics committee may approve the project as presented, require changes before it can start, or refuse approval altogether. Many committees have a further role of monitoring projects that are underway to ensure that the researchers fulfil their obligations and they can if necessary stop a project because of serious unexpected adverse events.

The reason why ethics committee approval of a project is required is that neither researchers nor research subjects are always knowledgeable and objective enough to determine whether a project is scientifically and ethically appropriate. Researchers need to demonstrate to an impartial expert committee that the project is worthwhile, that they are competent to conduct it, and that potential research subjects will be protected against harm to the greatest extent possible.

One unresolved issue regarding ethics committee review is whether a multi-centre project requires committee approval at each centre or whether approval by one committee is sufficient. If the centres are in different countries, review and approval is generally required in each country.

## Scientific Merit

"...medical research involving human subjects must be justifiable on scientific grounds"

Paragraph 11 of the **DoH** requires that medical research involving human subjects must be justifiable on scientific grounds. This requirement is meant to eliminate projects that are unlikely to succeed, for example, because they are methodologically inadequate, or that, even if successful, will likely produce trivial results. If patients are being asked to participate in a research project, even where risk of harm is minimal, there should be an expectation that important scientific knowledge will be the result.

To ensure scientific merit, paragraph 11 requires that the project be based on a thorough knowledge of the literature on the topic and on previous laboratory and, where appropriate, animal research that gives good reason to expect that the proposed intervention will be efficacious in human beings. All research on animals must conform to ethical guidelines that minimize the number of animals used and prevent unnecessary pain. Paragraph 15 adds a further requirement – that only scientifically qualified persons should conduct research on human subjects. The ethics review committee needs to be convinced that these conditions are fulfilled before it approves the project.

## Social Value

> "...social value has emerged as an important criterion for judging whether a project should be funded."

One of the more controversial requirements of a medical research project is that it contribute to the well-being of society in general. It used to be widely agreed that advances in scientific knowledge were valuable in themselves and needed no further justification. However, as resources available for medical research are increasingly inadequate, social value has emerged as an important criterion for judging whether a project should be funded.

Paragraphs 18 and 19 of the DoH clearly favour the consideration of social value in the evaluation of research projects. The importance of the project's objective, understood as both scientific and social importance, should outweigh the risks and burdens to research subjects. Furthermore, the populations in which the research is carried out should benefit from the results of the research. This is especially important in countries where there is potential for unfair treatment of research subjects who undergo the risks and discomfort of research while the drugs developed as a result of the research only benefit patients elsewhere.

The social worth of a research project is more difficult to determine than its scientific merit but that is not a good reason for ignoring it. Researchers, and ethics review committees, must ensure that patients are not subjected to tests that are unlikely to serve any useful social purpose. To do otherwise would waste valuable health resources and weaken the reputation of medical research as a major contributing factor to human health and well-being.

## Risks and Benefits

"If the risk is entirely unknown, then the researcher should not proceed with the project until some reliable data are available"

Once the scientific merit and social worth of the project have been established, it is necessary for the researcher to demonstrate that the risks to the research subjects are not unreasonable or disproportionate to the expected benefits of the research, which may not even go to the research subjects. A risk is the potential for an adverse outcome (harm) to occur. It has two components: (1) the likelihood of the occurrence of harm (from highly unlikely to very likely), and (2) the severity of the harm (from trivial to permanent severe disability or death). A highly unlikely risk of a trivial harm would not be problematic for a good research project. At the other end of the spectrum, a likely risk of a serious harm would be unacceptable unless the project provided the only hope of treatment for terminally ill research subjects. In between these two extremes, paragraph 17 of the DoH requires researchers to adequately assess the risks and be sure that they can be managed. If the risk is entirely unknown, then the researcher should not proceed with the project until some reliable data are available, for example, from laboratory studies or experiments on animals.

## Informed Consent

The first principle of the **Nuremberg Code** reads as follows: "The voluntary consent of the human subject is absolutely essential." The explanatory paragraph attached to this principle

> "The voluntary consent of the human subject is absolutely essential."

requires, among other things, that the research subject "should have sufficient knowledge and comprehension of the elements of the subject matter involved as to enable him to make an understanding and enlightened decision."

The **DoH** goes into some detail about informed consent. Paragraph 22 specifies what the research subject needs to know in order to make an informed decision about participation. Paragraph 23 warns against pressuring individuals to participate in research, since in such circumstances the consent may not be entirely voluntary. Paragraphs 24 to 26 deal with research subjects who are unable to give consent (minor children, severely mentally handicapped individuals, unconscious patients). They can still serve as research subjects but only under restricted conditions.

The **DoH**, like other research ethics documents, recommends that informed consent be demonstrated by having the research subject sign a 'consent form' (paragraph 22). Many ethics review committees require the researcher to provide them with the consent form they intend to use for their project. In some countries these forms have become so long and detailed that they no longer serve the purpose of informing the research subject about the project. In any case, the process of obtaining informed consent does not begin and end with the form being signed but must involve a careful oral explanation of the project and all that participation in it will mean to the research subject. Moreover, research subjects should be informed that they are free to withdraw their consent to participate at any time, even after the project has begun, without any sort of reprisal from the researchers or other physicians and without any compromise of their healthcare.

## Confidentiality

As with patients in clinical care, research subjects have a right to privacy with regard to their personal health information. Unlike clinical care, however, research requires the disclosure of personal health information

> "...research subjects have a right to privacy with regard to their personal health information"

to others, including the wider scientific community and sometimes the general public. In order to protect privacy, researchers must ensure that they obtain the informed consent of research subjects to use their personal health information for research purposes, which requires that the subjects are told in advance about the uses to which their information is going to be put. As a general rule, the information should be de-identified and should be stored and transmitted securely. The WMA **Declaration on Ethical Considerations Regarding Health Databases** provides further guidance on this topic.

## Conflict of Roles

It was noted earlier in this chapter that the physician's role in the physician-patient relationship is different from the researcher's role in the researcher-research subject relationship, even if the physician and the researcher are the same person. Paragraph 28 of the **DoH** specifies that in such cases, the physician role must take precedence. This means, among other things, that the physician must be prepared to recommend that the patient not take part in a research project if the patient seems to be doing well with the current treatment and the project requires that patients be randomized to different treatments and/or to a placebo. Only if the physician, on solid scientific grounds, is truly uncertain whether the patient's current treatment is as suitable as a proposed new treatment, or even a placebo, should the physician ask the patient to take part in the research project.

## Honest Reporting of Results

It should not be necessary to require that research results be reported accurately, but unfortunately there have been numerous recent accounts of dishonest practices in the publication of research results. Problems include *plagiarism*, data fabrication, duplicate publication and 'gift' authorship. Such practices may benefit the researcher, at least until they are discovered, but they can cause great harm to patients, who may be given incorrect treatments based on inaccurate or false research reports, and to other researchers, who may waste much time and resources trying to follow up the studies.

> "...there have been numerous recent accounts of dishonest practices in the publication of research results"

## Whistle-blowing

In order to prevent unethical research from occurring, or to expose it after the fact, anyone who has knowledge of such behaviour has an obligation to disclose this information to the appropriate authorities. Unfortunately, such whistle-blowing is not always appreciated or even acted on, and whistle-blowers are sometimes punished or avoided for trying to expose wrong-doing. This attitude seems to be changing, however, as both medical scientists and government regulators are seeing the need to detect and punish unethical research and are beginning to appreciate the role of whistle-blowers in achieving this goal.

Junior members of a research team, such as medical students, may find it especially difficult to act on suspicions of unethical research, since they may feel unqualified to judge the actions of senior researchers and will likely be subject to punishment if they speak out. At the very least, however, they should refuse to participate in practices that they consider clearly unethical, for example, lying to research subjects or fabricating data. If they observe others engaging in such practices, they should take whatever steps they can to alert relevant authorities, either directly or anonymously.

## Unresolved Issues

Not all aspects of research ethics enjoy general agreement. As medical science continues to advance, in areas such as genetics, the neurosciences and organ and tissue transplantation, new questions arise regarding the ethical acceptability of techniques, procedures and treatments for which

> "...only 10% of global research funding is spent on health problems that affect 90% of the world's population"

there are no ready-made answers. Moreover, some older issues are still subjects of continuing ethical controversy, for example, under what conditions should a placebo arm be included in a clinical trial and what continuing care should be provided to participants in medical research. At a global level, the 10/90 gap in medical research (only 10% of global research funding is spent on health problems that affect 90% of the world's population) is clearly an unresolved ethical issue. And when researchers do address problems in resource-poor areas of the world, they often encounter problems due to conflicts between their ethical outlook and that of the communities where they are working. All these issues will require much further analysis and discussion before general agreement is achieved.

Despite all these potential problems, medical research is a valuable and rewarding activity for physicians and medical students as well as for the research subjects themselves. Indeed, physicians and medical students should consider serving as research subjects so that they can appreciate the other side of the researcher-research subject relationship.

## BACK TO THE CASE STUDY

Dr. R should not have accepted so quickly. She should first find out more about the project and ensure that it meets all the requirements for ethical research.

In particular, she should ask to see the protocol that was submitted to the ethics review committee and any comments or conditions that the committee put on the project. She should only participate in projects in her area of practice, and she should satisfy herself about the scientific merit and social value of the project. If she is not confident in her ability to evaluate the project, she should seek the advice of colleagues in larger centres. She should ensure that she acts in the best interests of her patients and only enrols those who will not be harmed by changing their current treatment to the experimental one or to a placebo. She must be able to explain the alternatives to her patients so they can give fully informed consent to participate or not to participate. She should not agree to enrol a fixed number of patients as subjects since this could lead her to pressure patients to agree, perhaps against their best interests. She should carefully monitor the patients in the study for unexpected adverse events and be prepared to adopt rapid corrective action.

Finally, she should communicate to her patients the results of the research as they become available.

medical ethics

Medyczna etyka

medisinsk etikk

medizinische Ethik

# CHAPTER SIX –
# CONCLUSION

**Man Hiking on Steep Incline**
© Don Mason/CORBIS

## RESPONSIBILITIES AND PRIVILEGES
## OF PHYSICIANS

This Manual has focused on the duties and responsibilities of physicians, and indeed that is the main substance of medical

> "...like all human beings, physicians have rights as well as responsibilities"

ethics. However, like all human beings, physicians have rights as well as responsibilities, and medical ethics would be incomplete if it did not consider how physicians should be treated by others, whether patients, society or colleagues. This perspective on medical ethics has become increasingly important as physicians in many countries are experiencing great frustration in practising their profession, whether because of limited resources, government and/or corporate micro-management of healthcare delivery, sensationalist media reports of medical errors and unethical physician conduct, or challenges to their authority and skills by patients and other healthcare providers.

Medical ethics has in the past considered the rights of physicians as well as their responsibilities. Previous codes of ethics such as the 1847 version of the American Medical Association's Code included sections on the obligations of patients and of the public to the profession. Most of these obligations are outmoded, for example, "The obedience of a patient to the prescriptions of his physician should be prompt and implicit. He should never permit his own crude opinions as to their fitness, to influence his attention to them." However, the statement, "The public ought... to entertain a just appreciation of medical qualifications... [and] to afford every encouragement and facility for the acquisition of medical education...," is still valid. Rather than revising and updating these sections, however, the AMA eventually eliminated them from its Code of Ethics.

Over the years the WMA has adopted several policy statements on the rights of physicians and the corresponding responsibilities of others, especially governments, to respect these rights:

- The 1984 **Statement on Freedom to Attend Medical Meetings** asserts that "there should… be no barriers which will prevent physicians from attending meetings of the WMA, or other medical meetings, wherever such meetings are convened."

- The 1986 **Declaration on Physician Independence and Professional Freedom** states, "Physicians must have the professional freedom to care for their patients without interference" and "Physicians must have the professional freedom to represent and defend the health needs of patients against all who would deny or restrict needed care for those who are sick or injured."

- The 1995 **Statement on Professional Responsibility for Standards of Medical Care** declares that "any judgement on a doctor's professional conduct or performance must incorporate evaluation by the doctor's professional peers who, by their training and experience, understand the complexity of the medical issues involved." The same statement condemns "any procedures for considering complaints from patients or procedures for compensating patients, which fail to be based upon good faith evaluation of the doctor's actions or omissions by the physician's peers."

- The 1997 **Declaration Concerning Support for Medical Doctors Refusing to Participate in, or to Condone, the Use of Torture or Other Forms of Cruel, Inhuman or Degrading Treatment** commits the WMA "to support and protect, and to call upon its National Medical Associations to support and protect, physicians who are resisting involvement in such inhuman procedures or who are working to treat and rehabilitate victims thereof, as well as to secure the right to uphold the highest ethical principles including medical confidentiality...."

- The 2003 **Statement on Ethical Guidelines for the International Recruitment of Physicians** calls on every country to "do its utmost to retain its physicians in the profession as well as in the country by providing them with the support they need to meet their personal and professional goals, taking into account the country's needs and resources" and to ensure that "Physicians who are working, either permanently or temporarily, in a country other than their home country… be treated fairly in relation to other physicians in that country (for example, equal opportunity career options and equal payment for the same work)."

> "...physicians sometimes need also to be reminded of the privileges they enjoy."

Although such advocacy on behalf of physicians is necessary, given the threats and challenges listed above, physicians sometimes need also to be reminded of the privileges they enjoy. Public surveys in many countries have consistently shown that physicians are among the most highly regarded and trusted occupational groups. They generally receive higher than average remuneration (much higher in some countries). They still have a great deal of clinical autonomy, although not as much as previously. Many are engaged in an exciting search for new knowledge through participation in research. Most important, they provide services that are of inestimable value to individual patients, particularly those who are vulnerable and most in need, and to society in general. Few occupations have the potential to be more satisfying than medicine, considering the benefits that physicians provide – relief of pain and suffering, cure of illnesses, and comfort of the dying. Fulfilment of their ethical duties may be a small price to pay for all these privileges.

# RESPONSIBILITIES TO ONESELF

This Manual has classified physicians' ethical responsibilities according to their main beneficiaries: patients, society, and colleagues (including other health professionals). Physicians often forget that they have responsibilities to themselves, and to their families, as well. In many parts

> "Physicians often forget that they have responsibilities to themselves, and to their families, as well."

of the world, being a physician has required devoting oneself to the practice of medicine with little consideration for one's own health and well-being. Working weeks of 60-80 hours are not uncommon and vacations are considered to be unnecessary luxuries. Although many physicians seem to do well in these conditions, their families may be adversely affected. Other physicians clearly suffer from this pace of professional activity, with results ranging from chronic fatigue to substance abuse to suicide. Impaired physicians are a danger to their patients, with fatigue being an important factor in medical mishaps.

The need to ensure patient safety, as well as to promote a healthy lifestyle for physicians, is being addressed in some countries by restrictions on the number of hours and the length of shifts that physicians and trainees may work. Some medical educational institutions now make it easier for female physicians to interrupt their training programmes for family reasons. Although measures such as these can contribute to physician health and well-being, the primary responsibility for self-care rests with the individual physician. Besides avoiding such obvious health hazards as smoking, substance abuse and overwork, physicians should protect and enhance their own health and well-being by identifying stress factors in their professional and personal lives and by developing and practising appropriate coping strategies. When these fail, they should seek help from colleagues and appropriately qualified professionals for personal problems that might adversely affect their relationships with patients, society or colleagues.

## THE FUTURE OF MEDICAL ETHICS

This Manual has focussed on the current state of medical ethics, although with numerous references to its past. However, the present is constantly slipping away and it is necessary to anticipate the future if we are not to be always behind the times. The future of medical ethics will depend in large part on the future of medicine. In the first decade of the 21$^{st}$ century, medicine is evolving at a very rapid pace and it is difficult to predict how it will be practised by the time today's first-year medical students complete their training, and impossible to know what further changes will take place before they are ready to retire. The future will not necessarily be better than the present, given widespread political and economic instability, environmental degradation, the continuing spread of HIV/AIDS and other potential epidemics. Although we can hope that the benefits of medical progress will eventually spread to all countries and that the ethical problems they will face will be similar to those currently being discussed in the wealthy countries, the reverse could happen – countries that are wealthy now could deteriorate to the point where their physicians have to deal with epidemics of tropical diseases and severe shortages of medical supplies.

Given the inherent unpredictability of the future, medical ethics needs to be flexible and open to change and adjustment, as indeed it has been for some time now. However, we can hope that its basic principles will remain in place, especially the values of compassion, competence and autonomy, along with its concern for fundamental human rights and its devotion to professionalism. Whatever changes in medicine occur as a result of scientific developments and social, political and economic factors, there will always be sick people needing cure if possible and care always. Physicians have traditionally provided these services along with others such as health promotion, disease prevention and health system management. Although the balance among these activities may change in the future, physicians will likely continue to play an important role in all of them. Since each activity involves many ethical challenges, physicians will need to keep informed about developments in medical ethics just as they do in other aspects of medicine.

This is the end of the Manual but for the reader it should be just one step in a life-long immersion in medical ethics. To repeat what was stated in the Introduction, this Manual provides only a basic introduction to medical ethics and some of its central issues. It is intended to give you an appreciation of the need for continual reflection on the ethical dimension of medicine, and especially on how to deal with the ethical issues that you will encounter in your own practice. The list of resources provided in Appendix B can help you deepen your knowledge of this field.

# APPENDIX A - GLOSSARY

*Accountable* – answerable to someone for something (e.g., employees are accountable to their employers for the work they do). *Accountability* requires being prepared to provide an explanation for something one has done or has not done.

*Advance directive* – a statement, usually in writing, that indicates how a person would want to be treated, or not treated, if they are no longer able to make their own decisions (for example, if they are unconscious or demented). It is one form of advance care planning; another is choosing someone to act as one's substitute decision-maker in such situations. Some states have legislation on advance directives.

*Advocate* – (verb) to speak out or take action on behalf of another person or group; (noun) someone who acts in this way. Physicians serve as advocates for their patients when they call on governments or health insurance officials to provide services that their patients need but cannot easily obtain on their own.

*Anaesthetist* – in some countries the title, *anaesthesiologist*, is used instead.

*Beneficence* – literally, 'doing good'. Physicians are expected to act in the best interests of their patients.

*Bioethics/biomedical ethics* – two equivalent terms for the study of moral issues that occur in medicine, healthcare and the biological sciences. It has four major subdivisions: **clinical ethics**, which deals with issues in patient care (cf. Chapter Two of this Manual); **research ethics**, which deals with the protection of human subjects in healthcare research (cf. Chapter Five of this Manual); **professional ethics**, which deals with the specific duties and responsibilities that are required of physicians and other healthcare professions (**medical ethics** is one type of professional ethics); and **public policy ethics**, which deals with the formulation and interpretation of laws and regulations on bioethical issues.

*Consensus* – general, but not necessarily unanimous, agreement.

*Hierarchy* – an orderly arrangement of people according to different levels of importance from highest to lowest. *Hierarchical* is the adjective describing such an arrangement. The term, hierarchy, is also used to refer to the top leaders of an organization.

*Justice* – fair treatment of individuals and groups. As Chapter Three points out, there are different understandings of what constitutes fair treatment in healthcare.

*Managed healthcare* – an organizational approach to healthcare in which governments, corporations or insurance companies decide what services will be provided, who will provide them (specialist physicians, general practitioner physicians, nurses, other health professionals, etc.), where they will be provided (clinics, hospitals, the patient's home, etc.), and other related matters.

*Non-maleficence* – literally, not doing wrong. Physicians and medical researchers are to avoid inflicting harm on patients and research subjects.

*Palliative care* – an approach to the care of patients, especially those who are likely to die in the relatively near future from serious, incurable disease, that focuses on the patient's quality of life, especially pain control. It can be provided in hospitals, special institutions for dying patients (commonly called hospices), or in the patient's home.

*Physician* – an individual who is qualified to practise medicine. In some countries, physicians are distinguished from surgeons, and the term 'doctor' is used to designate both. However, 'doctor' is used by members of other health professions, such as dentists and veterinarians, as well as by all those who have obtained a Ph.D. or other 'doctoral' degree. The term 'medical doctor' is more precise but not widely used. The WMA uses the term 'physician' for all those who are qualified to practise medicine, no matter what their specialty, and this Manual does the same.

*Plagiarism* – a form of dishonest behaviour whereby a person copies the work of someone else, for example, all or part of a published article, and submits it as if it were the person's own work (i.e., without indicating its source).

*Pluralistic* – having several or many different approaches or features: the opposite of singular or uniform.

*Profess* – to state a belief or a promise in public. It is the basis of the terms 'profession', 'professional' and 'professionalism'.

*Rational* – based on the human capacity for reasoning, i.e., to be able to consider the arguments for and against a particular action and to make a decision as to which alternative is better.

*Surrogate or substitute gestation* – a form of pregnancy in which a woman agrees to gestate a child and give it up at birth to another individual or couple who in most cases have provided either the sperm (via artificial insemination) or the embryo (via in vitro fertilization and embryo transfer).

*Value* – (verb) to consider something to be very important; (noun) something that is considered to be very important.

*Virtue* – a good quality in people, especially in their character and behaviour. Some virtues are particularly important for certain groups of people, for example, compassion for physicians, courage for fire-fighters, truthfulness for witnesses, etc.

*Whistle-blower* – someone who informs people in authority or the public that an individual or an organization is doing something unethical or illegal. (The expression comes from the world of sport, where a referee or umpire blows a whistle to signal an infraction of the rules.)

# APPENDIX B – MEDICAL ETHICS RESOURCES ON THE INTERNET

## General

World Medical Association Policy Handbook (www.wma.net/e/policy/handbook.htm) – contains the full text of all WMA policies (in English, French and Spanish)

World Medical Association Ethics Unit (www.wma.net) – includes the following sections, updated monthly:

- Issue of the month
- WMA ethics outreach activities
- WMA ethics policies, including those in development or under review
- Declaration of Helsinki, history and current status
- WMA ethics resources
- Medical ethics organizations, including their codes of ethics
- Conference announcements
- Medical ethics education
- Ethics and human rights
- Ethics and medical professionalism.

## Beginning-of-life issues

Human cloning – www.who.int/ethics/topics/cloning/en/
Assisted reproduction – www.who.int/reproductive-health/infertility/report_content.htm

## End-of-life issues

Resources – www.nih.gov/sigs/bioethics/endoflife.html
Education for Physicians on End-of-life Care – www.ama-assn.org/ama/pub/category/2910.html
Palliative care – www.hospicecare.com/Ethics/ethics.htm
Opposition to euthanasia – www.euthanasia.com/

## HIV/AIDS

Resources – www.wits.ac.za/bioethics/
UNAIDS – www.unaids.org/en/in+focus/hiv_aids_human_rights/
unaids+activities+hr.asp

## Relations with commercial enterprises

Educational resources – www.ama-assn.org/ama/pub/category/5689.html
Resources – www.nofreelunch.org/

## Research on human subjects

Guidelines and resources – www.who.int/ethics/research/en/
Harvard School of Public Health, ethical issues in international health
research course – www.hsph.harvard.edu/bioethics/

# APPENDIX C

## WORLD MEDICAL ASSOCIATION

### Resolution on the Inclusion of Medical Ethics and Human Rights in the Curriculum of Medical Schools World-Wide

(Adopted by the 51st World Medical Assembly,
Tel Aviv, Israel, October 1999)

1. Whereas Medical Ethics and Human Rights form an integral part of the work and culture of the medical profession, and

2. Whereas Medical Ethics and Human Rights form an integral part of the history, structure and objectives of the World Medical Association,

3. It is hereby resolved that the WMA strongly recommend to Medical Schools world-wide that the teaching of Medical Ethics and Human Rights be included as an obligatory course in their curricula.

## WORLD FEDERATION FOR MEDICAL EDUCATION (WFME):

### Global Standards for Quality Improvement – Basic Medical Education
(www.sund.ku.dk/wfme/Activities/Translations%20of%20Standard%20Doc uments/WFME%20Standard.pdf)

These standards, which all medical schools are expected to meet, include the following references to medical ethics:

1.4 Educational Outcome

The medical school **must** define the competencies (including knowledge and understanding of medical ethics) that students should exhibit on graduation in relation to their subsequent training and future roles in the health system.

4.4 Educational Programme – Medical Ethics

The medical school **must** identify and incorporate in the curriculum the contributions of medical ethics that enable effective communication, clinical decision-making and ethical practices.

4.5 Educational Programme – Clinical Sciences and Skills

Clinical skills include history taking, communication and team leadership skills.

Participation in patient care would include teamwork with other health professions.

## 4.4 Educational Resources – Research

The interaction between research and education activities **should** encourage and prepare students to engage in medical research and development.

# APPENDIX D - STRENGTHENING ETHICS TEACHING IN MEDICAL SCHOOLS

Some medical schools have very little ethics teaching while others have highly developed programs. Even in the latter ones, however, there is always room for improvement. Here is a process that can be initiated by anyone, whether medical student or faculty member, who wants to strengthen the teaching of medical ethics in his or her institution.

1. Become familiar with the decision-making structure in the institution
   - Dean
   - Curriculum Committee
   - Faculty Council
   - Influential faculty members

2. Seek support from others
   - Students
   - Faculty
   - Key administrators
   - National medical association
   - National physician regulatory body

3. Make a strong case
   - WMA *Resolution on the Inclusion of Medical Ethics and Human Rights in the Curriculum of Medical Schools World-Wide*
   - WFME *Global Standards for Quality Improvement – Basic Medical Education*
   - Examples from other medical schools
   - Research ethics requirements
   - Anticipate objections (e.g., overcrowded curriculum)

4. Offer to help
   - Provide suggestions for structure, content, faculty and student resources (cf. WMA Ethics Unit web page on medical ethics education resources: www.wma.net/e/ethicsunit/education.htm
   - Liase with other medical ethics programmes, the WMA, etc.

5. Ensure continuity
   - Advocate for a permanent medical ethics committee
   - Recruit younger students
   - Recruit additional faculty
   - Engage new faculty and key administrators

**APPENDIX E - ADDITIONAL CASE STUDIES**

## CONTRACEPTIVE ADVICE
## TO A TEENAGER

Sara is 15 years old. She lives in a town where sexual assaults are becoming more and more frequent. She comes to your clinic asking for a prescription for oral contraceptives to protect her from pregnancy in case she is the victim of a sexual assault. Pregnancy would terminate her education and make it very difficult to find a husband. Sara tells you that she does not want her parents to know that she will be using contraceptives because they will think that she intends to have sex with a boyfriend. You are suspicious of Sara's motives but you admire her determination to avoid pregnancy.

You advise her to come to the clinic with her parents for a general discussion of the issue with you. Three days later she returns alone and tells you that she tried to speak to her parents about the issue but they refused to discuss it.

Now what should you do?

# A PREMATURE INFANT*

Max was born during the 23rd week of pregnancy. He is ventilated because his lungs are very immature. Moreover, he suffers from cerebral bleeding because his vessel tissue is still unstable. It is unlikely that he will actually survive the next few weeks. If he does, he will probably be severely handicapped both mentally and physically.

Max's condition worsens when he develops a serious infection of the bowel. It might be possible to extract the inflamed part of the bowel operatively, which would preserve his small chance of survival. His parents refuse to consent because they do not want Max to suffer from the operation and they feel that his quality of life will never be sufficient. As the treating physician you think that the operation should be done, and you wonder how to deal with the parents' refusal.

* Suggested by Dr. Gerald Neitzke and Ms. Mareike Moeller, Medizinische Hochschule Hannover, Germany

## HIV INFECTION*

Mr. S is married and the father of two school children. He is treated in your clinic for a rare form of pneumonia that is often associated with AIDS. His blood test results show that he is indeed HIV-positive. Mr. S says that he wants to decide himself if and when he will tell his wife about the infection. You indicate that it could be life-saving for his wife to protect herself from infection. Besides, it would be important for her to have an HIV test herself. In case of a positive test result she would then have the opportunity to take drugs to slow down the outbreak of the disease and thereby prolong her life. Six weeks later, Mr. S comes into your clinic for a control investigation. Answering your question he says that he hasn't informed his wife yet. He doesn't want her to know about his homosexual contacts because he fears that she would end their relationship and the family would shatter. But to protect her he has had only "safer sex" with her. As the treating physician, you wonder whether you should inform Mrs. S of the HIV status of her husband against his will so that she would have the opportunity to start treatment if needed.

# TREATING A PRISONER

As part of your medical duties you spend one day every two weeks seeing inmates in a nearby prison. Yesterday you treated a prisoner with multiple abrasions on his face and trunk. When you asked what caused the injuries, the patient replied that he had been attacked by prison staff during interrogation when he refused to answer their questions. Although this is the first such case you have experienced, you have heard of similar cases from your colleagues. You are convinced that you should do something about the problem but the patient refuses to authorize you to disclose information about himself for fear of retaliation from the prison authorities. Furthermore, you are not certain that the prisoner has told you the truth; the guard who brought him to you said that he had been in a fight with another prisoner.

You have a good relationship with the prison staff and do not want to harm it by making unsubstantiated accusations of mistreatment of prisoners. What should you do?

## END-OF-LIFE DECISION

An 80-year old woman is admitted to your hospital
from a nursing home for treatment of pneumonia.
She is frail and mildly demented. You treat the
pneumonia successfully but just before she is to be
discharged back to the nursing home, she suffers
a stroke that leaves her paralysed on her right
side and unable to feed herself. A feeding tube
is inserted that apparently causes her discomfort
and after she has made several attempts to pull
it out with her left arm, a restraint is placed on
the arm. She is otherwise unable to express her
wishes. A search for children or other relatives who
could help make decisions about her treatment is
unsuccessful. After several days you conclude that
her condition is unlikely to improve and that the
only ways to relieve her suffering are to sedate
her or to withdraw the feeding tube and
allow her to die. What should you do?

# COLLECTIONS OF CASE STUDIES

UNESCO Chair in Bioethics informed consent case studies –http://research.haifa.ac.il/~medlaw/ (UNESCO Chair)

UK Clinical Ethics Network case studies – www.ethics-network.org.uk/Cases/archive.htm

Harvard School of Public Health international health research case studies – www.hsph.harvard.edu/bioethics/ (cases)

Commonwealth Medical Trust Training Manual of Ethical and Human Rights Standards for Healthcare Professionals, Part 3, case studies – www.commat.org/